Table of Contents

Message from Richard Cordray

Director of the CFPB

Last year, we delivered the first integrated view of the Consumer Financial Protection Bureau's (CFPB's or Bureau's) Strategic Plan for fiscal years 2013–2017, as well as the Budget and Annual Performance Plan and Report. This holistic presentation of the Bureau's goals, budget, performance measures, and accomplishments achieves our goal to increase transparency and make information accessible to American consumers and other key stakeholders, including Congress as well as Federal, and state agencies.

Building on the established integrated framework, we are presenting a comprehensive review of progress that the CFPB achieved in fiscal year (FY) 2013 across its four established Strategic Goals for FY 2013–2017. The document also contains the Bureau's most current view of budget projections for FY 2014–2015 and corresponding performance measures across the full set of performance goals.

To share a few highlights, in FY 2013, the CFPB:

- Launched 160 supervision activities at various financial institutions;

- Handled approximately 144,000 consumer complaints about credit cards, mortgages, and other financial products;

- Provided digital content, materials, and decision tools to over 1.9 million consumers;

- Established key infrastructure for the Civil Penalty Fund to distribute payments to identified victims.

These accomplishments clearly signal that the Bureau maintains an unwavering focus on leveraging available resources wisely and carefully. The CFPB remains committed to data-driven and objective decision-making processes, as well as the robustness, completeness, and reliability of performance information.

Congress created this independent bureau within the Federal Reserve System as part of the Dodd-Frank Wall Street Reform and Consumer Protection Act of 2010 in direct response to a severe financial crisis. The Bureau is dedicated to fulfilling its consumer protection mission by providing research insights, making sound policy, delivering informational resources, and overseeing financial markets. The CFPB will continue to work closely with Congress, businesses, consumer advocates, and its Federal, state, and local partners to strengthen accountability for consumer financial protection.

Sincerely,

Richard Cordray, Director
March 2014

Overview of the CFPB

The Bureau of Consumer Financial Protection, known as the Consumer Financial Protection Bureau (CFPB), was established on July 21, 2010 under Title X of the Dodd-Frank Wall Street Reform and Consumer Protection Act Public Law No. 111-203 (Dodd-Frank Act). The CFPB was established as an independent bureau within the Federal Reserve System. The Bureau is an Executive agency as defined in Section 105 of Title 5, United States Code.

The Dodd-Frank Act authorizes the CFPB to exercise its authorities to ensure that, with respect to consumer financial products and services:

1. Consumers are provided with timely and understandable information to make responsible decisions about financial transactions;

2. Consumers are protected from unfair, deceptive, or abusive acts and practices and from discrimination;

3. Outdated, unnecessary, or unduly burdensome regulations are regularly identified and addressed in order to reduce unwarranted regulatory burdens;

4. Federal consumer financial law is enforced consistently in order to promote fair competition; and

5. Markets for consumer financial products and services operate transparently and efficiently to facilitate access and innovation.

Under the Dodd-Frank Act, on the designated transfer date, July 21, 2011, certain authorities and functions of several agencies relating to Federal consumer financial law transferred to the CFPB in order to accomplish the above objectives. These authorities were transferred from the Board of Governors of the Federal Reserve System (Board of Governors), Office of the Comptroller of the Currency (OCC), Office of Thrift Supervision (OTS), Federal Deposit Insurance Corporation (FDIC), National Credit Union Administration (NCUA), and the Department of Housing and Urban Development (HUD). In addition, Congress vested the Bureau with authority to enforce in certain circumstances the Federal Trade Commission's (FTC) Telemarketing Sales Rule and its rules under the FTC Act, although the FTC retains full authority over these rules. The Dodd-

Frank Act also provided the CFPB with certain other Federal consumer financial regulatory authorities.

Our organization

Under the Dodd-Frank Act, the Secretary of the Treasury was responsible for establishing the CFPB and performing certain functions of the Bureau until a Director of the CFPB was in place. The Bureau's day-to-day operations were managed by the Special Advisor to the Secretary of the Treasury for the Consumer Financial Protection Bureau until January 4, 2012, when President Obama recess appointed Richard Cordray as the first Director of the CFPB. Subsequently, the U.S. Senate confirmed the appointment of Richard Cordray on July 16, 2013, and Director Cordray was sworn in as the first Senate confirmed Director of the CFPB on July 17, 2013.

To accomplish its mission, the CFPB is organized into six primary divisions:

1. **Consumer Education and Engagement:** works to empower consumers with the knowledge, tools, and capabilities they need in order to make better-informed financial decisions by engaging them in the right moments of their financial lives, while addressing the unique financial challenges faced by four specific populations.

2. **Supervision, Enforcement and Fair Lending:** ensures compliance with Federal consumer financial laws by supervising market participants and bringing enforcement actions when appropriate.

3. **Research, Markets and Regulations:** conducts research to understand consumer financial markets and consumer behavior, evaluates whether there is a need for regulation, and determines the costs and benefits of potential or existing regulations.

4. **Legal Division:** ensures the Bureau's compliance with all applicable laws and provides advice to the Director and the Bureau's divisions.

5. **External Affairs:** manages the Bureau's relationships with external stakeholders and ensures that the Bureau maintains robust dialogue with interested stakeholders to promote understanding, transparency, and accountability.

6. **Operations:** builds and sustains the CFPB's operational infrastructure to support the entire organization and hears directly from consumers about challenges they face in the marketplaces through their complaints, questions, and feedback.

Our mission

The CFPB is a 21st century agency that helps consumer finance markets work by making rules more effective, by consistently and fairly enforcing those rules, and by empowering consumers to take more control over their economic lives.

Our vision

If we achieve our mission, then we will have encouraged the development of a consumer finance marketplace

- where customers can see prices and risks up front and where they can easily make product comparisons;

- in which no one can build a business model around unfair, deceptive, or abusive practices;

- that works for American consumers, responsible providers, and the economy as a whole.

We will achieve our mission and vision through:

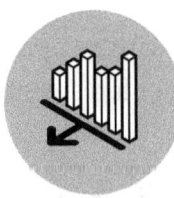

Data-driven analysis

The CFPB is a data-driven agency. We take in data, manage it, store it, share it appropriately, and protect it from unauthorized access. Our aim is to use data purposefully, to analyze and distill data to enable informed decision-making in all internal and external functions.

Innovative use of technology

Technology is core to the CFPB accomplishing its mission. This means developing and leveraging technology to enhance the CFPB's reach, impact, and effectiveness. We strive to be recognized as an innovative, 21st century agency whose approach to technology serves as a model within government.

Valuing the best people and great teamwork

At the CFPB, we believe our people are our greatest asset. Therefore, we invest in world-class training and support in order to create a diverse and inclusive environment that encourages employees at all levels to tackle complex challenges. We also believe effective teamwork extends outside the walls of the CFPB. We seek input from and collaborate with consumers, industry, government entities, and other external stakeholders.

We aim to embody the following values in everything we do:

Service

Our mission begins with service to the consumer and our country. We serve our colleagues by listening to one another and by sharing our collective knowledge and experience.

Leadership

Fostering leadership and collaboration at all levels is at the core of our success. We believe in investing in the growth of our colleagues and in creating an organization that is accountable to the American people.

Innovation

Our organization embraces new ideas and technology. We are focused on continuously improving, learning, and pushing ourselves to be great.

Plan overview

Our strategic plan articulates four goals

Goal 1	Prevent financial harm to consumers while promoting good practices that benefit them.
Goal 2	Empower consumers to live better financial lives.
Goal 3	Inform the public, policy makers, and the CFPB's own policy-making with data-driven analysis of consumer finance markets and consumer behavior.
Goal 4	Advance the CFPB's performance by maximizing resource productivity and enhancing impact.

In support of each goal we outline

Budget	Resource allocations we will make in order to achieve our goals.
Outcomes	Desired outcomes that further define the focus of our work.
Strategies & investments	Strategies and investments that lay out the actions we will take to accomplish our outcomes.
Performance goals	Specific, measurable goals we will use to assess our progress along with associated measures and indicators.

Budget overview

The CFPB's operations are funded principally by transfers made by the Board of Governors of the Federal Reserve System from the combined earnings of the Federal Reserve System, up to the limits set forth in the Dodd-Frank Act. The Director of the CFPB requests transfers from the Federal Reserve System in amounts that he has determined are reasonably necessary to carry out the Bureau's mission without exceeding the limits in the Dodd-Frank Act. Transfers through FY 2013 are capped at set percentages of the total 2009 operating expenses of the Federal Reserve System. In fiscal years 2014 and beyond, the cap is adjusted annually based on the percentage increase in the employment cost index for the total compensation for State and local government workers published by the Federal Government. Transfers from the Federal Reserve System are capped at $608.4 million for FY 2014. For FY 2015, the funding cap is currently estimated to be $618.7 million. Funds transferred from the Federal Reserve System are deposited into the Bureau of Consumer Financial Protection Fund (Bureau Fund), which is maintained at the Federal Reserve Bank of New York.

Pursuant to the Dodd-Frank Act, the CFPB is also authorized to collect and retain for specified purposes civil penalties obtained from any person for violations of Federal consumer financial laws. The CFPB generally is authorized to use these funds for payments to the victims of activities for which civil penalties have been imposed, and may also use the funds for consumer education and financial literacy programs under certain circumstances. Funds collected by the CFPB under this authority are deposited into the Consumer Financial Civil Penalty Fund (Civil Penalty Fund) maintained at the Federal Reserve Bank of New York.

Bureau Fund

The CFPB FY 2014 and FY 2015 budget estimates included in this report will support the operations of the Bureau while it continues to grow and mature as a Federal agency. These resources will enable the Bureau to continue to fulfill its statutory obligations and its mission to make rules more effective, by consistently and fairly enforcing those rules, and by empowering consumers to take more control over their financial lives.

The FY 2015 budget estimate of $583.4 million is 2.4% above the FY 2014 budget level of $569.8 million. The budget supports ongoing operations, additional examiner staff, and key investments, especially in developing the consumer response system and other IT infrastructure projects, to achieve the four strategic goals outlined in this plan.

Budget by strategic goal

Goal 1	Prevent financial harm to consumers while promoting good practices that benefit them.
Goal 2	Empower consumers to live better financial lives.
Goal 3	Inform the public, policy makers, and the CFPB's own policy-making with data-driven analysis of consumer finance markets and consumer behavior.
Goal 4	Advance the CFPB's performance by maximizing resource productivity and enhancing impact.

The data below provides a view of our budgetary resources by strategic goal. The proportion of funding across all goals is expected to remain relatively constant through FY 2015. Activities related to regulation, supervision, and enforcement activities, which are included in Goal 1, represent the largest proportion of the budget at 47% and primarily support the continued growth of the regional supervision and examination workforce as the CFPB moves towards steady-state levels. Other key investments in FY 2014 and FY 2015 are devoted to activities under Goal 2, which include expanding capacity and systems to improve the handling and processing of consumer complaints as well as helping consumers understand the costs, risks, and trade-offs of financial decisions through financial education outreach tools, and support.

The proportion of funding for Goal 3 and 4 decreases through FY 2015 as research and market monitoring functions as well as investments in human capital and internal infrastructure begin reaching maturity.

TABLE 1:   Budget by strategic goal

	FY 2013	%	FY 2014	%	FY 2015	%
Goal 1	$231,428,989	43%	$266,316,370	47%	$275,217,834	47%
Goal 2	$111,886,226	21%	$123,560,303	22%	$133,662,241	23%
Goal 3	$58,521,214	11%	$58,436,996	10%	$56,022,179	10%
Goal 4	$136,896,529	25%	$121,531,078	21%	$118,515,946	20%
Total	$538,732,958	100%	$569,844,747	100%	$583,418,201	100%

* FY 2014 and FY 2015 estimates are based on the best available information at the time the budget was prepared and are subject to revision.

** FY 2013 amounts reflect obligations incurred and include upward adjustments to prior year obligations.

Budget by program

Over the FY 2014–FY 2015 time period, the budget provides additional resources for all programs. Supervision, Enforcement, and Fair Lending primarily drive the increases in funding over this two-year window to support additional staff and systems development, such as e-tools that enhance the ability to assess compliance with Federal consumer financial laws.

Consumer Response realizes a significant increase in funding in FY 2014 and FY 2015 as it continues to process increased volumes of complaints and seek new ways to improve existing processes to make them as efficient, effective, and easy-to-use as possible. From FY 2012 to FY 2013, the volume of consumer complaints handled by the Bureau grew by 94.6%. By FY 2015, the Bureau expects the number of complaints to continue to grow as consumers increasingly utilize the variety of tools, programs, and initiatives that provide targeted, meaningful, and accessible assistance and information. This projected increase in handling complaints is described in more detail under the discussion of Goal 2.

Within Operations, personnel and investments in technology drive the rise in funding in FY 2014. In FY 2015, increased funding to support staffing will continue, but will be partially offset by technological developments entering a more steady state.

In addition to enterprise-wide administrative and operational costs (e.g. building space, rent, utilities), Centralized Services in FY 2014 also includes one-time investments supporting a relocation of CFPB employees to a temporary building during the second half of FY 2014 in preparation of major building renovations to the current D.C. headquarters building. Funding for the building renovations is included in FY 2013 Centralized Services as the result of an inter-agency agreement between the General Services Administration (GSA) and the CFPB. The current headquarters building has not undergone a significant renovation since it was constructed in 1976. Planned renovations include replacement of major utilities and infrastructure such as the roof, building enclosure, and heating, water, and electrical systems. Once the Bureau moves to the temporary location, it expects to see cost reductions in FY 2015 related to the discontinuation of regular maintenance and operating costs of the current D.C. headquarters during the relocation.

Funding changes for Consumer Education and Engagement as well as Research, Markets, and Regulations are due to the variety of key investments and their respective life cycle stages. These are detailed in the Summary of Key Investments table and in each goal discussion.

TABLE 2: Budget by program

	FY 2013	FY 2014	FY 2015
Office of the Director	$5,234,704	$4,515,983	$4,711,724
Operations	$54,171,404	$68,684,285	$69,744,184
Operations - Consumer Response	$39,586,117	$68,782,620	$73,072,513
Consumer Education and Engagement	$22,263,284	$31,589,071	$38,588,426
Research, Markets, and Regulation	$32,895,564	$47,815,380	$42,556,406
Supervision, Enforcement, and Fair Lending	$105,568,127	$165,342,969	$174,770,999
Legal	$10,308,644	$15,508,793	$16,891,971
External Affairs	$4,833,964	$6,909,993	$7,807,621
Other Programs*	$1,241,727	$3,310,693	$3,611,304
Centralized Services**	$262,629,424	$157,384,960	$151,663,053
Total	**$538,732,958**	**$569,844,747**	**$583,418,201**

* Other Programs include the Director's Financial Analyst Program, Ombudsman, and Administrative Law Judges.

** Centralized Services include the cost of certain administrative and operational services provided centrally to other programs (e.g., building space, utilities, and IT-related equipment and services).

FTE by program

The table below reflects full-time equivalent employees (FTEs) by program. The Bureau will continue to expand capacity over FY 2013 levels in order to successfully achieve its strategic goals. More than 45% of the growth in staff over the next two fiscal years will support the Supervision, Enforcement, and Fair Lending Division, while the Bureau continues to staff its regional examination workforce. The Bureau will also continue to increase FTE levels in Consumer Response in order to ensure sufficient capacity to handle the increasing volume of consumer complaints. Planned staffing in the Operations program offices will continue to support the Bureau's development of the internal infrastructure, critical to creating and maintaining a high-performing organization. More detail on personnel investments is included in each discussion by goal.

TABLE 3: FTE by program

Programs	FY 2013	FY 2014	FY 2015
Office of the Director	27	27	28
Operations	221	304	325
Consumer Response	134	191	223
Consumer Education and Engagement	55	73	77
Research, Markets, and Regulations	107	147	156
Supervision, Enforcement, and Fair Lending	527	742	834
Legal	51	70	76
External Affairs	29	44	47
Other Programs	11	26	30
Total	1,162	1,624	1,796

Budget by object class

The table below provides a view of the CFPB's budget by spending category or object classification. Personnel compensation and benefits represent the largest increases over the two-year horizon as the Bureau continues to hire additional personnel as described above. Total travel expenses are also projected to increase over time as the examination workforce continues to grow and conduct various examination activities across the country. The growth in funds allocated to rents, communications, and miscellaneous charges represent the costs related to temporarily relocating CFPB employees during the renovation of the D.C. headquarters, which is scheduled to begin in the latter part of FY 2014.

The FY 2014 increase in funding for other for "Other Contractual Services" and "Equipment" indicates various technology investments that support the continued development of IT infrastructure throughout the Bureau. Lower budget estimates in these categories in FY 2015 reflect the short-term nature of these investments.

TABLE 4: Budget by object classification

Object Classification	FY 2013	FY 2014	FY 2015
Personnel Compensation	$143,341,164	$203,079,639	$234,551,540
Personnel Benefits	$48,998,214	$69,575,962	$79,940,993
Benefits to Former Personnel	$70,856	$223,381	$282,990
Travel and Transportation of Persons	$14,484,205	$22,555,217	$26,129,269
Transportation of Things	$154,148	$25,000	$30,000
Rents, Communications, and Misc Charges	$5,611,501	$12,775,278	$17,622,000
Printing and Reproduction	$2,227,637	$2,007,011	$2,943,411
Other Contractual Services	$136,790,301	$215,081,450	$185,154,321
Supplies and Materials	$4,659,968	$4,806,891	$4,934,321

Object Classification	FY 2013	FY 2014	FY 2015
Equipment	$31,586,601	$39,714,918	$31,829,356
Land and Structures	$150,805,839	-	-
Interest and Dividends	$2,523	-	-
Total	$538,732,958	$569,844,747	$583,418,201

Summary of key investments

Since FY 2013, the CFPB has expanded the activities associated with key investments in order to achieve its strategic goals. The table below details the funding levels for the Bureau's key non-personnel investments by outcome. Spending for certain investments, such as IT infrastructure, supervision compliance tools, e-law tools for supervision and enforcement activities, and operational improvements in the consumer response system, will increase in FY 2014, but decrease in FY 2015 as start-up costs decline. Spending on investments, such as audits of the Bureau, the consumer response contact center, and litigation support, will continue at similar levels in FY 2014 and FY 2015. Other investments, such as the consumer experience program and underserved populations research and innovations, reflect funding at increased levels in FY 2014 and FY 2015 as the CFPB continues its work to promote a healthy consumer financial marketplace and provide consumers with the information and tools to improve their financial lives. Key investments are presented in more detail in the discussion of each goal.

TABLE 5: Key investments (in millions)

Outcome	Key Investment Description	FY 2013	FY 2014	FY 2015
1.1	Disclosure, design, testing and implementation	$0.4	$3.4	$0.3
1.2, 1.3	Examiner training and travel	$12.1	$21.9	$24.2
	Supervision compliance tool	$5.0	$7.5	$4.5
	E-law tools and support	$4.6	$12.6	$8.4
	Litigation support	$2.1	$3.0	$3.5
	Mortgage servicing project	–	$3.0	$3.0
	Supervision and examination system	–	$1.1	$1.1
2.1	Consumer response system and contact center support	$18.1	$22.7	$27.8
	Consumer response operational and program support	$3.7	$5.1	$2.6
	Optimizing CFPB communication and consumer engagement channels	$ 0.4	$2.7	$1.4
	Consumer response system - natural language processing	–	$10.7	$8.1
2.2	Consumer experience program	$3.9	$5.6	$6.8
	Consumer education campaigns	$1.7	$2.2	$2.5
	Underserved and special populations program	$0.9	$0.3	$0.9
	Underserved and special populations outreach	$0.7	$2.7	$7.6
	Optimizing CFPB communication and consumer engagement channels	$0.4	$0.8	–
	Your money, your goals	–	$0.7	$0.2
3.1	Credit card database	$4.1	$3.0	$3.0
	Other market data	$2.3	$1.4	$0.9

Outcome	Key Investment Description	FY 2013	FY 2014	FY 2015
	HMDA development and implementation	$2.3	$3.0	$2.5
	Evidence-based consumer financial market research	$0.4	$1.7	$0.5
	Mortgage database	$1.0	$1.1	$1.1
3.2	Compliance cost study	$2.0	–	–
	Financial education research	$1.9	$1.2	$1.4
	Underserved and special populations research	$0.9	$2.1	$2.0
	Consumer experience program	$0.8	$0.6	$0.6
	Financial education innovations	$0.7	$1.0	$1.0
	Evidence-based consumer financial market research	$0.2	$2.5	$0.3
	Financial education metrics	$0.1	$0.7	$1.4
	Know before you owe–mortgage closing	–	$2.0	$2.0
4.1	Human capital shared services, infrastructure, and operations	$8.6	$8.9	$9.7
	Learning, leadership, and organization development facilitation and design	$4.4	$4.9	$4.2
	Outreach, candidate recruiting, and candidate selection support	$1.3	$3.8	$2.7
4.2	Infrastructure	$31.9	$27.2	$19.4
	Design and software development support	$6.1	$5.6	$6.1
	Cybersecurity	$3.5	$3.5	$3.1
	Portfolio management	$0.2	$11.9	$11.6
	Data infrastructure and analysis	$1.2	$1.5	$0.7

Outcome	Key Investment Description	FY 2013	FY 2014	FY 2015
4.3	Audits of the Bureau	$11.7	$6.8	$6.8
	Financial management support services	$6.2	$6.5	$5.9
	Internal controls	$2.1	$1.5	$1.5
All	HQ building renovation	$145.1	–	–
	Facilities agreements (occupancy)	$16.5	$18.7	$17.2
	Facilities agreements (utilities, security, other)	$11.3	$12.2	$5.9
	Architecture and engineering services for HQ building renovation	$5.1	–	–
	Personnel security investigations	$1.1	$1.2	$1.4
	Facilities agreements (occupancy) for temporary space	–	$5.8	$10.0
	Facilities agreements (utilities, security, other) for temporary space	–	$10.1	$3.5
	Other*	$19.4	$40.6	$39.3
Total		$346.3	$297.0	$268.6

*Includes administrative costs such as training, supplies, printing, transportation, and programmatic costs as well as upward adjustments to prior year obligations.

Budget authority

Funding required to support the CFPB's operations is obtained primarily through transfers from the Board of Governors of the Federal Reserve System. Funding is capped at a set percentage of the total 2009 operating expenses of the Federal Reserve System, subject to an annual adjustment. Beginning in FY 2014, transfers to the Bureau are capped at 12 percent of the Federal Reserve System's operating expenses, but will be adjusted annually based on the percentage increase in the employment cost index for total compensation for State and local government workers published by the Federal Government as specified in the Dodd-Frank Act. The inflation-adjusted transfer cap for FY 2014 is $608.4 million, and the transfer cap for FY 2015 is currently estimated to be $618.7 million. Funds transferred from the Federal Reserve System to fund the operations of the Bureau are transferred into the Bureau Fund and maintained at the Federal Reserve Bank of New York. The Bureau anticipates requesting less than the transfer cap to fund operations in FY 2014 and FY 2015.

In addition to transfers from the Federal Reserve, a small portion of the CFPB's budget resources comes from receipts collected from interest on treasury securities and filing fees pursuant to the Interstate Land Sales Full Disclosure Act of 1968 (ILSA). ILSA fees are deposited into an account maintained by the Department of the Treasury and may be expended for the purpose of covering all or part of the costs that the Bureau incurs to operate the ILSA Program.

TABLE 6: Bureau Fund (in millions)

Receipts	FY 2013	FY 2014	FY 2015
Transfers from the Federal Reserve Board	$518.4	$561.3	$583.0
Other Receipts	$0.4	$0.4	$0.4
Unobligated Balances, start of year	$99.6	$88.1	$80.0
Recoveries of Prior Year Obligations	$8.8	–	–
Total Budgetary Resources	**$627.2**	**$649.8**	**$663.4**
Total Obligations	**$538.7**	**$569.8**	**$583.4**

Civil Penalty Fund budget authority

The Dodd-Frank Act authorizes the CFPB to collect and retain for specified purposes civil penalties obtained from any person in a judicial or administrative action under Federal consumer financial laws. The CFPB maintains the Consumer Financial Civil Penalty Fund (CPF) for this purpose. Collections of civil penalties are deposited into the CPF, and such funds are available for payments to victims of activities for which civil penalties have been imposed under the Federal consumer financial laws and, if victims cannot be located or payments are not practicable, the Bureau can use such funds for consumer education and financial literacy programs. As directed by the Dodd-Frank Act, the CFPB maintains a separate account for these funds at the Federal Reserve Bank of New York.

On May 7, 2013, the Bureau published the Civil Penalty Fund rule, 12 C.F.R. part 1075, a final rule governing how the Bureau will administer funds in the CPF. This rule states that the Civil Penalty Fund Administrator will allocate funds to classes of eligible victims and, as appropriate, to consumer education and financial literacy programs in accordance with a schedule published by the Bureau on its website.

The CFPB collected $81.5 million in actual deposits by the end of FY 2013 and expects to collect additional amounts during FY 2014. Of the amounts collected to date, the Bureau allocated $26.4 million as published in the CPF annual report[1]. Approximately $13.0 million was allocated to compensate harmed consumers and $13.4 million for consumer education and financial literacy programs. Of the $13.4 million allocated to consumer education and financial literacy programs, $4.5 million are planned to be obligated in FY 2014, $4.5 million in FY 2015, and $4.4 million in FY 2016.

Additional information regarding allocations from the CPF is available at consumerfinance.gov.

TABLE 7: Civil Penalty Fund (in millions)

Receipts	FY 2013	FY 2014	FY 2015
Collections	$49.5	$10.0	$0.3
Unobligated Balances, start of year	$32.0	$81.5	$74.0
Total Budgetary Resources	**$81.5**	**$91.5**	**$74.3**
Total Obligations	–	**$17.5**	**$4.5**

---

1 The Dodd-Frank Act requires the CFPB to publish an annual report of the Civil Penalty Fund. The Civil Penalty Fund Annual Report was published within the FY 2013 Financial Report of the Consumer Financial Protection Bureau, which is available at www.consumerfinance.gov.

Goal 1

Prevent financial harm to consumers while promoting good practices that benefit them.

TABLE 8:   Budget by program, goal 1

Goal 1	FY 2013	FY 2014	FY 2015
Office of the Director	$1,308,676	$1,128,996	$1,177,931
Research, Markets, and Regulation	$9,183,078	$15,827,979	$13,746,198
Supervision, Enforcement, and Fair Lending	$105,568,127	$165,342,969	$174,770,999
Legal	$3,711,112	$6,090,703	$6,776,617
External Affairs	$725,095	$1,036,499	$1,171,143
Other Programs	$613,303	$1,750,401	$1,980,440
Centralized Services	$110,319,599	$75,138,823	$75,594,506
Total	$231,428,989	$266,316,370	$275,217,834

FIGURE 1: Almost every American family relies on one or more financial products[2]

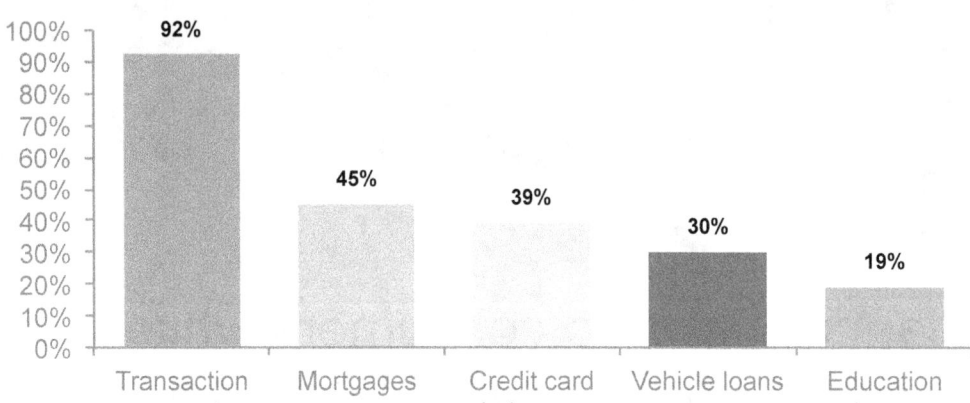

Prior to Congress enacting the Dodd-Frank Act, consumer financial protection had not been the primary focus of any one Federal agency, and no agency could set the rules for the entire financial market. The result was a system without sufficiently effective rules or consistent enforcement of the law. The absence of such a regulating entity and corresponding rules ultimately contributed to the 2008 financial crisis.

Consumer financial protection is the CFPB's singular focus. The Dodd-Frank Act increased accountability in government by consolidating consumer financial protection authorities that had existed across seven different Federal agencies into one, the newly formed Consumer Financial Protection Bureau. These authorities include the ability to issue regulations under more than a dozen Federal consumer financial laws. As provided in section 1021 of the Dodd-Frank Act, the purpose of the CFPB is to implement and enforce Federal consumer financial laws consistently for the purpose of ensuring that all consumers have access to markets for consumer financial products and services and that such markets are fair, transparent, and competitive.

In addition, the Dodd-Frank Act gives the CFPB the authority to supervise and examine many non-bank financial service providers previously unsupervised at the Federal level, such as mortgage companies, payday lenders, private education lenders, and larger debt collectors and consumer reporting companies. With the consolidation of existing and new authorities under one roof, the CFPB is now focused and equipped to prevent financial harm to consumers while promoting practices that benefit consumers across financial institutions.

---

2 Federal Reserve Board, "2010 Survey of Consumer Finances," tables 13–10, 6–10 based on public data, last updated 7/19/2012, http://www.Federalreserve.gov/econresdata/scf/scf_2010.htm (Last viewed 8/23/2012).

FIGURE 2: Financial institutions subject to CFPB supervisory authority for consumer financial protection purposes

Large banks, thrifts, credit unions & their affiliates	Certain nonbank institutions
Representing over $10 trillion in assets (~75% of total industry)	Including companies engaged in mortgage lending, brokering, and servicing; payday lenders; private education lenders; and larger participants of the consumer debt collection and consumer reporting markets

Industry structure is always changing, and therefore, so too will the number of institutions that fall under the CFPB's supervisory authority. The CFPB is designed to be agile and adjust its approach to supervising the financial industry in order to respond rapidly to changing consumer needs.

The CFPB will accomplish its first goal by achieving three outcomes

Outcome 1.1: *Create, adopt, and administer regulations in order to promote a consumer financial marketplace in which: (A) consumers can understand the costs, benefits, and risks associated with consumer financial products and services initially and over the term of the product or service, and (B) consumers are not subject to deceptive, unfair, abusive, or discriminatory practices.*

Outcome leader: Associate Director of Research, Markets, and Regulations

This outcome will be accomplished through the following strategies and investments:

Strategies

- Develop and maintain an efficient fact-based approach to developing, evaluating, revising, and finalizing regulations.

- Develop a rule-writing team with highly advanced skills in relevant and specialized legal and business areas.

- Work with consumers and industry stakeholders on developing regulations to implement existing Federal consumer financial laws effectively.

- Leverage technology to continuously improve the efficiency and effectiveness of the Federal rulemaking processes and procedures.

- Study electronic delivery of financial product disclosure information to consumers and develop methods to facilitate electronic delivery that will provide benefits to consumers and industry. Work with industry groups and other stakeholders to develop data standards or build on existing standards to facilitate electronic delivery of financial products to consumers, create new tools that help consumers understand the financial products they buy, and reduce unwarranted regulatory burden for industry.

Investments

PERSONNEL

Continue to expand capacity to conduct rulemaking activities, provide interpretive guidance, develop small business compliance guides and provide other implementation support, and evaluate benefits and costs of potential rules.

DISCLOSURE DESIGN, TESTING, AND IMPLEMENTATION

Continue to obtain and use expertise in disclosure design and disclosure usability testing. Qualitative research, such as one-on-one cognitive interviews, enables the Bureau to put forward proposed forms which consumers are more likely to be able to navigate and comprehend. The Bureau will also integrate these mortgage disclosure requirements under the Truth in Lending Act and Real Estate Settlement Procedures Act.

We will assess our progress through the following three performance goals:

Performance goal 1.1.1: Complete consumer protection related rulemakings within nine months of receipt of final public comments.

The Bureau has made it a priority to ensure that it puts consumer protection regulations into place, including those implementing statutory requirements, in a timely manner. For this reason, the Bureau believes that completion of its own regulatory proposals within nine months of the close of the public comment period is a good measure of whether it is meeting this goal.

PERFORMANCE MEASURE

TABLE 9: The percentage of proposed rulemakings, conducted solely by the CFPB, finalized or otherwise resolved within nine months of the due date for receipt of final public comments. [3]

	FY 2012	FY 2013	FY 2014	FY 2015
Target	NA	75%	75%	75%
Actual	100%	88%	NA	NA

PROGRESS UPDATE AND FUTURE ACTION

In FY 2013, the Bureau finalized a number of mortgage rules it proposed in FY 2012 to implement consumer protection provisions enacted by the Dodd-Frank Act. For example, in January 2013, the Bureau issued mortgage servicing rules under the Truth in Lending Act (TILA) and the Real Estate Settlement Procedures Act (RESPA), and issued a final rule under the TILA concerning loan originators' licensing and registration, training, screening, and compensation practices. In addition, the Bureau finalized rules amending Regulation B to implement the Dodd-Frank Act's disclosure and delivery requirements for copies of appraisals and other written valuations under the Equal Credit Opportunity Act (ECOA). The Bureau also issued a final rule amending Regulation Z to implement the Dodd-Frank Act's changes to the Home Ownership and Equity Protection Act (HOEPA) expanding the scope of HOEPA coverage and adding new consumer protections. This rule also implemented additional Dodd-Frank requirements relating to homeownership counseling requirements under the RESPA and the TILA. All of these rules were based on the Bureau's proposals issued in summer 2012. By issuing

---

3 This measure does not include interagency rulemakings, rulemakings inherited from the Federal Reserve Board, and rulemakings on which the Bureau expects to do further quantitative research following the receipt of public comments.

these and other final rules in January 2013 and meeting its statutory deadlines in addition to the strategic goals, the Bureau also demonstrated its commitment to timely issuance of regulations.

During FY 2013, the Bureau also issued a proposed and final rule modifying earlier remittances regulations that it had issued in 2012.[4] In addition, the Bureau issued a number of clarifying and technical amendments to the January 2013 mortgage rules. Going forward, early in FY 2014, the Bureau will finalize its proposed rulemaking to integrate certain mortgage disclosures under the RESPA and the TILA.

Performance goal 1.1.2: Complete all five-year regulation assessments on schedule.

Section 1022(d) of the Dodd-Frank Act requires the CFPB to assess each significant rule the Bureau adopts and publish a report of the assessment within five years of the effective date. The assessment addresses, among other factors, the rule's effectiveness in meeting the purposes and objectives of the Dodd-Frank Act, Title X and the specific goals the Bureau states for the rule.

PERFORMANCE MEASURE

The percentage of five-year regulation assessments completed on schedule.

Targets

FY 2012: N/A
FY 2013: Develop a plan for meeting a pre-rule baseline
FY 2014: Develop strategies to best isolate the effects of rules
FY 2015: Begin collection and analysis of relevant quantitative and qualitative information.

Actuals

FY 2013: The Bureau began identifying existing data that may be useful for establishing baselines and for analysis of potential changes from those baselines, identifying gaps in the necessary data, and planning for the acquisition of additional data to fill those gaps.

---

4 This rule amended the Bureau's February 2012 final remittance rule, which finalized a rulemaking initiated by the Federal Reserve Board.

PROGRESS UPDATE AND FUTURE ACTION

The Bureau's first five-year assessments will be due in 2018. The Bureau will in FY 2014 develop strategies to best isolate the effects of rules to enable the Bureau to conduct before-and-after reviews of certain rules.

Performance goal 1.1.3: Ensure that all rulemakings are informed by public outreach processes, such as Small Business Regulatory Enforcement Fairness Act (SBREFA) panels and consumer and industry roundtables.

The Regulatory Flexibility Act, as amended by SBREFA and the Dodd-Frank Act, requires the Bureau to convene a Small Business Review Panel before proposing a rule that will have a significant economic impact on a substantial number of small entities. Other public outreach efforts, such as meetings with consumers and industry stakeholders in the development of a proposal, inform and otherwise assist the Bureau in crafting more effective rules. The Bureau is also interested in exploring ways to increase general consumer involvement in the rulemaking process.

PERFORMANCE MEASURE

TABLE 10: The percentage of significant consumer protection related, notice-and-comment rulemakings informed by public outreach processes

	FY 2012	FY 2013	FY 2014	FY 2015
Target	NA	100%	100%	100%
Actual	100%	100%	NA	NA

PROGRESS UPDATE AND FUTURE ACTION

In January 2013, the CFPB finalized a number of proposed mortgage-related rules to implement consumer protection changes required by the Dodd-Frank Act. Those rules were informed in several cases by Small Business Review Panel meetings with small entities that had been conducted as required by SBREFA in 2012, as well as various other roundtables and meetings held both before and after the issuance of the proposed rules. In FY 2013, the CFPB also issued several proposed rules to amend, modify, or supplement its mortgage-related rules. Those proposals were informed by ongoing public outreach efforts to industry stakeholders and consumer advocates to monitor implementation issues in connection with the January 2013 mortgage rules, including a number of consumer and industry stakeholder roundtables and meetings and staff participation in numerous external events. These outreach efforts provided stakeholders an opportunity to provide input and discuss any issues presented by the implementation of the mortgage rules or other matters for the Bureau to consider as it formulated additional proposals. The CFPB also encouraged all stakeholders to submit formal written comments on its proposals.

In addition to conducting outreach efforts for mortgage-related rules, the CFPB held a number of other consumer and industry stakeholder outreach events and meetings in FY 2013 as it continued to consider and develop future consumer protection rules. In anticipation of possible future rulemaking or policy efforts, the Bureau held roundtables related to debt collection practices and plans to issue an advance notice of proposed rulemaking in FY 2014 seeking additional information from the public. The CFPB intends to continue to undertake its public outreach efforts to consumers and industry stakeholders as it considers topics for other possible future consumer protection related rules in FY 2014. For example, the Bureau will engage with the public and convene a Small Business Review Panel pursuant to SBREFA on a proposed rule involving the Home Mortgage Disclosure Act.

Outcome 1.2: *Supervise institutions to foster compliance with Federal consumer financial laws, promote a fair consumer financial marketplace, and prevent unlawful discrimination.*

Outcome 1.3: *Enforce Federal consumer financial laws and hold violators accountable.*

Outcome leader: Associate Director of Supervision, Enforcement, and Fair Lending

These outcomes will be accomplished through the following strategies and investments:

Strategies

- Acquire and analyze qualitative and quantitative information and data pertaining to consumer financial product and service markets and companies.

- Focus resources on institutions and their product lines that, based on their size, nature of the product, and field and market intelligence, pose the greatest risk to consumers.

- Implement a framework for sharing information, coordinating activity, and promoting best practices with fellow financial institution supervisory and law enforcement agencies to ensure the most effective use of regulatory resources.

- Implement internal policies that facilitate the integration of the Bureau's supervision, enforcement, and fair lending functions.

- Continue to develop a technology solution for coordinating supervisory information, capable of recording, storing, tracking, and reporting information on the CFPB's supervisory process.

- Continue implementing a tool capable of reviewing loan and deposit portfolios for compliance with Federal consumer financial laws.

Investments

PERSONNEL

Hire additional staff to expand the Bureau's capacity to focus on risks to consumers in the policies and practices of consumer financial providers; analyze available data on the activities of providers, on the markets in which they operate, and on the risks to consumers; implement and enforce Federal consumer financial laws consistently for both bank and nonbank consumer financial companies; and investigate and take actions to address potential violations of consumer laws.

EXAMINER TRAINING AND TRAVEL

Support the development and delivery of training courses that are essential to examiner commissioning and to maintaining a highly effective workforce. Also support the travel requirements of the Bureau's distributed workforce in order to effectively carryout its supervision program.

SUPERVISION COMPLIANCE TOOL

Automate data analysis in order to review loan files more thoroughly, use supervision resources more efficiently, and streamline the on-site portion of the exam. This tool will improve the Bureau's ability to assess compliance with Federal consumer financial laws, including fair lending laws, and assess and detect risks to consumers.

E-LAW TOOLS AND SUPPORT

Maintain and increase capacity of electronic tools that obtain, process, and analyze evidence received in enforcement investigations, enabling the Bureau to bring enforcement actions to address violations of Federal consumer financial laws more efficiently.

LITIGATION SUPPORT

Employ standard investigatory tools to compel documents and testimony and to seek injunctive and monetary remedies through civil actions or administrative proceedings. These functions require the use of services such as expert witnesses, court reporters, and transcription services.

MORTGAGE SERVICING PROJECT

Lay the groundwork for the development of systems to assist consumers during the loan modification process and collect and analyze information on loan servicer performance. Investments will inform the CFPB's efforts, particularly in the development of evaluative materials.

SUPERVISION AND EXAMINATION SYSTEM

Continue developing and implementing a replacement system that will organize entities by institution product line, capture relationships between entities, support supervisory workflows, and document the supervision process.

We will assess our progress through the following eight performance goals:

Performance goal 1.2.1 / 1.3.1: Perform supervision activities at financial services institutions under the CFPB's jurisdiction to foster compliance with Federal consumer financial laws.

The CFPB's Supervision Examinations, Supervision Policy, Enforcement, and Fair Lending Offices collaborate to conduct supervisory activities at bank and nonbank institutions. The CFPB's supervisory authority includes banks, thrifts, and credit unions with over $10 billion in assets, and their affiliates, as well as certain nonbank consumer financial service providers, such as mortgage lenders, brokers, and servicers; private education lenders; payday lenders; and larger participants of the consumer reporting and debt collection markets. These supervisory activities will foster compliance with Federal consumer financial laws, promote a fair consumer financial marketplace, and prevent unlawful discrimination.

Performance measure

TABLE 11: Supervision activities opened during the fiscal year

	FY 2012	FY 2013	FY 2014	FY 2015
Actual	149	160	NA	NA

PROGRESS UPDATE AND FUTURE ACTION

In FY 2013, the Bureau continued to implement its supervision program, opening 160 supervisory actions during FY 2013 at large banks and nonbank financial institutions. These activities included continuing existing supervision programs across product areas including mortgage origination, mortgage servicing, credit cards, deposits, student lending, and short-term, small dollar loans. They also included the first ever review of consumer reporting agencies and nonbank debt collectors.

The CFPB expanded its Supervision and Examination Manual by adding chapters on:

- Debt collection examination procedures (October 2012),

- Education loan examination procedures (December 2012),

- Truth in Lending Act interim procedures (June 2013)

- Equal Credit Opportunity Act (ECOA) interim procedures (appraisal and valuation requirements) (June 2013)

- ECOA baseline review procedures (July 2013)

- Real Estate Settlement Procedures Act interim procedures (August 2013)

- Short-term, small-dollar lending procedures (September 2013)

The Bureau also continued to coordinate with Federal and state regulators to minimize unnecessary regulatory burden, avoid unnecessary duplication of effort, and decrease the risk of conflicting supervisory directives. In May 2013, the Bureau entered into a framework with state financial regulatory authorities that established a dynamic and flexible process for coordination on supervision and enforcement matters.

Throughout FY 2013, the Bureau also focused on continuing to recruit and hire the staff to execute the work of the supervision program. These efforts included hiring of additional 114 examiners across the country and completing the permanent hiring of all four Regional Directors. The CFPB also made significant investments to build out the Washington, D.C.

infrastructure, training programs, and systems which contribute to supporting a national examination force. In FY 2014, the CFPB will continue to grow its diverse and talented team to accomplish the goals of the supervision program.

Performance goal 1.2.2 / 1.3.2: Effectively initiate supervisory activities at financial services institutions under the CFPB's jurisdiction to determine compliance with the Federal fair lending laws, including the Equal Credit Opportunity Act (ECOA) and the Home Mortgage Disclosure Act (HMDA).

The CFPB's fair lending supervision program assesses whether supervised entities have engaged in, or are engaging in, violations of the Federal fair lending laws. We accomplish this assessment through examinations that evaluate institutions' compliance with those laws.

PERFORMANCE MEASURE

TABLE 12: Fair lending supervision activities opened during the fiscal year[5]

	FY 2012	FY 2013	FY 2014	FY 2015
Actual	67	47	NA	NA

PROGRESS UPDATE AND FUTURE ACTION

In FY 2013, the Bureau continued its data-driven fair lending supervision operations, opening 10 new Targeted ECOA Exams (focusing on auto and mortgage lending) and 37 new HMDA Data Integrity Exams.

To increase the transparency of CFPB supervisory processes, the Bureau published the ECOA Baseline Review Modules, which are used by CFPB examination teams when conducting ECOA Baseline Reviews. The Bureau also prepared its HMDA Resubmission Schedule and Guidelines, released in early October 2013 (FY 2014), which provide instruction and additional details on the HMDA Data Integrity Examination process.

---

5 The indicator above counts mortgage Targeted ECOA Exams and their associated HMDA Data Integrity Exams separately as two examinations. The overall supervision activities indicator combines mortgage Targeted ECOA Exams and its associated HMDA Data Integrity Exam as a single examination.

Performance goal 1.2.3 / 1.3.3: Issue examination reports within the CFPB's established time periods following the close of examinations.

Effective supervision of financial institutions to foster compliance with Federal consumer financial laws requires prompt notice to institutions of matters requiring their attention and action to avoid further violations or consumer harm. A thorough report development and review process ensures high-quality reports that appropriately explain what the examination team found and why corrective actions, if any, are required.

PERFORMANCE MEASURE

TABLE 13: Percentage of examination reports issued within an established period following the close of the examination

	FY 2012	FY 2013	FY 2014	FY 2015
Target	NA	Baseline	50%	60%
Actual	NA	15%	NA	NA

PROGRESS UPDATE AND FUTURE ACTION

The CFPB is focused on issuing high-quality examination reports in a timely manner. The established time period for issuance of reports will be refined as the CFPB continues to examine more institutions (both bank and nonbank) and our review process is refined. To that end, the CFPB recently initiated a comprehensive evaluation of the report review process at both the headquarters and regional levels. The initial review findings were released to CFPB senior leadership in December 2013 with implementation of recommendations scheduled to begin in the second quarter of FY 2014. Even after recommended improvements are implemented, the CFPB will continue to review and analyze its processes to determine methods for improvement and increased effectiveness and efficiency.

Performance goal 1.2.4 / 1.3.4: Supervisory matters requiring attention resolved by the prescribed timeframe.

The CFPB monitors institutions receiving notice of matters requiring attention to ensure that corrective actions are taken by the prescribed timeframe in response to supervisory activities, which foster compliance with Federal consumer financial laws and promote a fair consumer financial marketplace.

PERFORMANCE MEASURE

The percentage of supervisory matters requiring attention resolved by the prescribed timeframe in response to supervisory activities.

TABLE 14: The percentage of supervisory matters requiring attention resolved by the prescribed timeframe in response to supervisory activities

	FY 2012	FY 2013	FY 2014	FY 2015
Target	NA	Baseline	80%	80%
Actual	NA	62%	NA	NA

PROGRESS UPDATE AND FUTURE ACTION

The CFPB regions responsible for supervised institutions have given notice to institutions of any matters requiring attention resulting from supervisory activities and are monitoring responses by these institutions. The CFPB will conduct on-site reviews of particular issues or actions that may require independent validation.

The CFPB has and will continue to issue Supervisory Highlights several times per year, through which it will apprise the public and the financial services industry about its examination program, including the concerns that it finds during the course of its completed work, and the remedies that it obtains for consumers who have suffered financial or other harm. The CFPB believes that Supervisory Highlights will help providers of financial products and services better understand the CFPB's supervisory expectations so that they can take action to comply with Federal consumer financial laws and serve their customers in a fair and transparent way.

The CFPB intends to be transparent about the goals of its supervision program and the steps being taken to achieve those goals, while protecting the confidentiality of the underlying financial institution-specific information. In FY 2014, CFPB plans to enhance its ability to monitor and track the progress of supervisory matters requiring attention by building an automated tracking capacity into our Supervisory and Examinations System (SES).

Performance goal 1.2.5 / 1.3.5: Cooperate and share information with its partners in local, state, and Federal law enforcement as part of its efforts to protect consumers, deter wrongdoers, and build a better marketplace.

This indicator ensures that the CFPB works well with its partners at the local, state, and Federal level to share information, subject to the Bureau's regulations and policies on information sharing, across jurisdictions and to make the best use of limited resources.

PERFORMANCE MEASURE

TABLE 15: Cases in which the CFPB obtains information from local, state, or Federal law enforcement partners that contributes to CFPB law enforcement actions, or investigations in which the CFPB cooperates or shares information with law enforcement partners

	FY 2012	FY 2013	FY 2014	FY 2015
Actual	22	80	NA	NA

PROGRESS UPDATE AND FUTURE ACTION

The Bureau continues to cultivate strong working relationships with its partners at Federal, state, and local regulators and law enforcement agencies. The Bureau has signed MOUs with the Conference of State Bank Supervisors and other signatories from all 50 states, plus Puerto Rico and the District of Columbia, in order to intake the Nationwide Mortgage Licensing System and the Mortgage Call Report, and to preserve the confidentiality of any information shared between the parties. In May 2013, the Bureau entered into a framework with state financial regulatory authorities that established a dynamic and flexible process for coordination on supervision and enforcement matters. In December 2012, the Bureau signed an MOU with the Department of Justice to strengthen coordination on fair lending enforcement and avoid duplication of their respective Federal law enforcement efforts. The Bureau has also signed approximately 40 other information-sharing MOUs with Federal, state, and local governmental agencies. For example, the Office of Enforcement, as well as the Office of Consumer Response, contribute data to the FTC's Consumer Sentinel, which is available to local, state, and Federal law enforcement entities across the country.

The Bureau has shared investigative information with more than 50 different government agencies since opening its doors and will continue to coordinate and cooperate with its partners in our efforts to protect consumers. The Bureau is committed to maximizing its ability to protect and assist consumers through its partners while also ensuring that confidential information relating to consumers and businesses is appropriately protected.

Performance goal 1.2.6 / 1.3.6: Where the Bureau determines enforcement action is warranted, file or settle action within two years of opening its investigation.

Filing enforcement actions in a timely manner is an important measure of the CFPB's effectiveness. The Bureau seeks to balance the need to effectively pursue complex and time-consuming cases while minimizing any unnecessary delay between conduct and resolution. Timely pursuit of resolutions increases deterrence and provides consumers with greater protections of law.

PERFORMANCE MEASURE

TABLE 16: Where the Bureau determines enforcement action is warranted, file or settle action within two years of opening its investigation

	FY 2012	FY 2013	FY 2014	FY 2015
Target	NA	Baseline	Baseline	TBD
Actual	NA	Baseline under development	NA	NA

PROGRESS UPDATE AND FUTURE ACTION

Following the determination that enforcement action is warranted, each matter is reviewed at regular intervals to ensure that it is progressing in a timely manner. Because the CFPB opened its doors on July 21, 2011, not enough time will have elapsed by September 30, 2014, to form a complete baseline from which to measure the percentage of enforcement actions that were filed within two years of the Bureau's determination that enforcement action was warranted. Therefore, targets will be established in the future.

In FY 2013, the Office of Enforcement rolled out a series of measures that better enabled tracking of the timeliness of actions. It also continued to meet hiring goals and to complete development of policies and infrastructures that enable it to investigate and take action efficiently and effectively. For example, in FY 2013, the Bureau issued and sought comment on an interim final rule on the Rules of Practice for Issuance of Temporary Cease and Desist Orders. The Bureau also issued significant guidance with regard to the following areas related to enforcement: responsible business conduct and the importance of self-policing, self-reporting, remediation, and cooperation; unfair, deceptive, or abusive acts or practices in the collection of consumer debts; indirect auto lending and compliance with the Equal Credit Opportunity Act; and representations regarding the effect of debt payments on credit scores.

Performance goal 1.2.7 / 1.3.7: Successfully resolve the cases the CFPB files in court and administrative adjudicative proceedings whether by litigation, settlement, issuance of a default judgment, or other means.

This measure ensures that the CFPB successfully resolves as many actions as possible while, at the same time, pursuing complex and challenging actions when appropriate, even when success is not assured.

PERFORMANCE MEASURE

TABLE 17: The percentage of all cases filed by the CFPB that were successfully resolved through litigation, a settlement, issuance of a default judgment, or other means

	FY 1012	FY 2013	FY 2014	FY 2015
Target	NA	75%	75%	75%
Actual	100%	100%	NA	NA

PROGRESS UPDATE AND FUTURE ACTION

In FY 2012, all of the enforcement matters were successfully resolved. In FY 2013, the Office of Enforcement obtained monetary relief for more than 2.4 million consumers, including redress in excess of $414 million and civil money penalties totaling more than $50 million. These actions included an order requiring one of the nation's largest banks to refund an estimated $309 million to more than 2.1 million customers for illegal credit card practices. This enforcement action was the result of work started by the Office of the Comptroller of the Currency (OCC), which the CFPB joined last year. The Bureau also obtained orders for $6.5 million in restitution for servicemembers from another major bank and one of its nonbank partner companies. Those companies were also ordered to stop targeting active-duty military with deceptive marketing and auto-lending practices.

The Office of Enforcement also secured the Bureau's first two favorable court decisions in litigated enforcement actions, resulting in permanent injunctions against two companies and their operators who were taking advantage of consumers through foreclosure relief schemes, and orders for the defendants to pay more than $13 million in restitution for their victims. In addition, the Bureau resolved significant actions against debt relief companies that misled consumers and charged illegal fees for services they often failed to provide.

Finally, the Bureau obtained more than $15.4 million in penalties from four mortgage insurers who had been paying unlawful kickbacks to lenders in exchange for business referrals. In FY 2014 and beyond, the Bureau will seek to continue to successfully resolve cases.

Performance goal 1.2.8 / 1.3.8: Successfully resolve the fair lending cases the CFPB files in court and administrative adjudicative proceedings, whether by litigation, settlement, issuance of a default judgment, or other means.

When the Dodd-Frank Act created within the CFPB an Office of Fair Lending, it set forth as one of that Office's functions the enforcement of Federal fair lending laws, including ECOA and HMDA. The CFPB seeks to successfully resolve as many fair lending actions as possible while, at the same time, pursuing complex and challenging actions when appropriate, even when success is not assured.

PERFORMANCE MEASURE

TABLE 18: The percentage of all fair lending cases filed by the CFPB that were successfully resolved through litigation, a settlement, issuance of a default judgment, or other means

	FY 2012	FY 2013	FY 2014	FY 2015
Target	NA	75%	75%	75%
Actual	100%	NA[6]	NA	NA

PROGRESS UPDATE AND FUTURE ACTION

In FY 2013, the Bureau worked on two key public enforcement actions announced in early October 2013 (FY 2014) against Bureau-supervised home mortgage lenders related to HMDA and Regulation C. The Bureau ordered one bank and one nonbank to pay civil money penalties ($34,000 and $425,000, respectively) for violating HMDA, which requires certain mortgage lenders to accurately collect and report data about mortgage loan applications. The entities also were required to correct and resubmit HMDA data and develop and implement an effective HMDA compliance management system to prevent future violations. In FY 2014 and beyond, the Bureau will seek to continue to successfully resolve fair lending cases.

---

6 Although the stipulations for the two public enforcement actions were executed in September 2013, the denominator for this goal is zero because the consent orders were executed in October 2013, and the result is "N/A". These two matters will count as successfully resolved in the FY14 results.

Goal 2

Empower consumers to live better financial lives.

The CFPB works to empower consumers with the knowledge, tools, and capabilities they need in order to make better-informed financial decisions by engaging them in the right moments of their financial lives, in moments when they are most receptive to seeking out and acting on assistance. To that end, the CFPB will develop and maintain a variety of tools, programs, and initiatives that provide targeted, meaningful, and accessible assistance and information to consumers at the moment they need it, both directly and through others who reach consumers directly.

TABLE 19: Budget by program, goal 2

Goal 2	FY 2013	FY 2014	FY 2015
Office of the Director	$1,308,676	$1,128,996	$1,177,931
Operations– Consumer Response	$39,586,117	$68,782,620	$73,072,513
Consumer Education, and Engagement	$16,977,742	$23,055,667	$28,716,706
Legal	$721,605	$1,145,348	$1,254,734
External Affairs	$725,095	$1,036,499	$1,171,143
Other Programs	$41,502	$135,867	$147,388
Centralized Services	$52,525,490	$28,275,305	$28,121,826
Total	**$111,886,226**	**$123,560,303**	**$133,662,241**

FIGURE 3: While almost all Americans are impacted by financial products,[7]

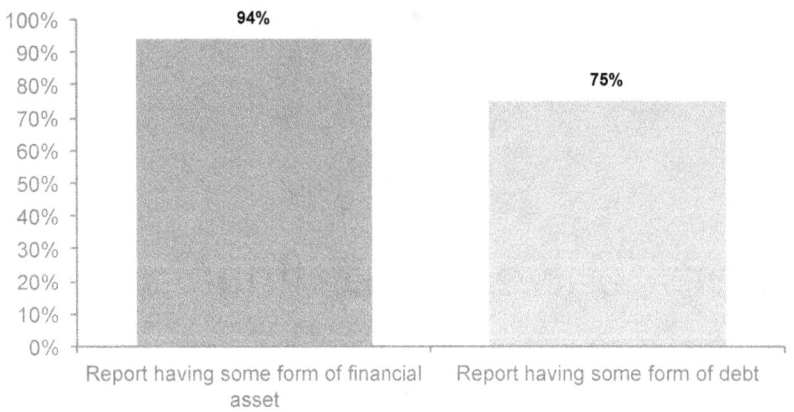

FIGURE 4: Many face challenges in making financial decisions.[8]

19%	of individuals reported that over the past year, their household spent more than their income.
60%	of individuals lack a rainy day fund to cover expenses even for three months in case of emergencies.
61%	of individuals said that, when obtaining their most recent credit card, they did not collect and compare information about cards from more than one company.

Differences in financial education, capabilities, and skills contribute to this problem. Consumers represent diverse populations with diverse financial needs, choices, and challenges; they seek out information about financial choices using a variety of channels. Therefore, the CFPB must be flexible and adaptable in addressing the highly diverse needs of American consumers. We can accomplish this by ensuring that our workforce reflects the faces, ideas, backgrounds and experiences of the American public.

---

7 Federal Reserve Board, "Changes in U.S. Family Finances from 2007 to 2010: Evidence from the Survey of Consumer Finances," Federal Reserve Bulletin, Vol 98, No 2, June 2012, pp. 28, 61, http://www.federalreserve.gov/pubs/bulletin/2012/pdf/scf12.pdf (Last viewed 8/23/2012).

8 FINRA 2012 Investor Education Foundation's Financial Capability Study, http://www.usfinancialcapability.org (Last viewed 1/23/2014).

FIGURE 5: Percentage of American families obtaining information about borrowing or investing through various sources[9]

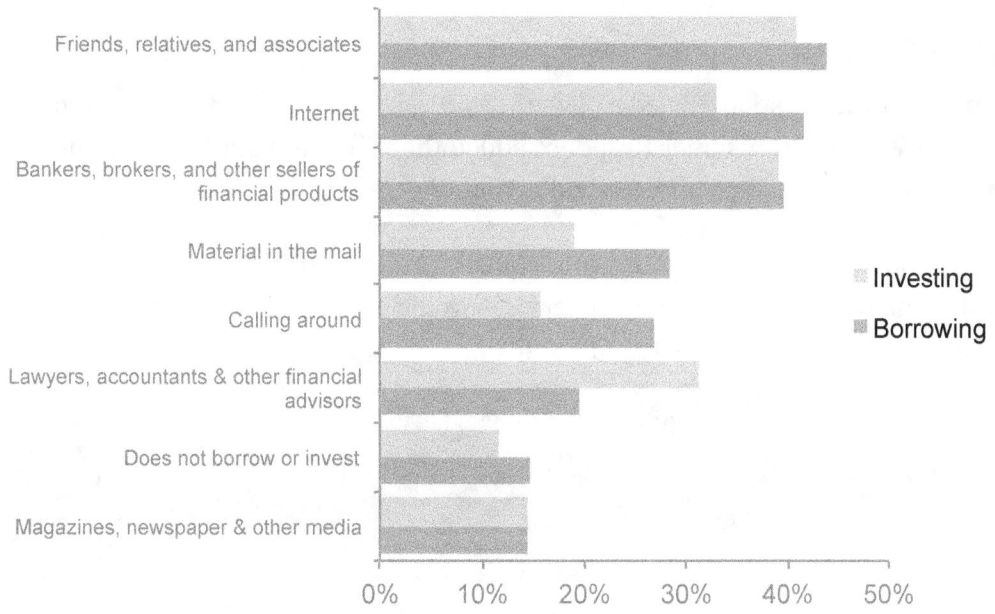

The CFPB will accomplish its second goal by achieving two outcomes

Outcome 2.1: *Collect, monitor, respond to and share data associated with consumer complaints and inquiries regarding consumer financial products or services.*

Outcome leader: Associate Director, Operations

The CFPB provides direct assistance to consumers, in real time, through its Office of Consumer Response. Consumer Response hears directly from consumers about the challenges they face in

9 Federal Reserve Board, "Changes in U.S. Family Finances from 2007 to 2010: Evidence from the Survey of Consumer Finances," Federal Reserve Bulletin, Vol 98, No 2, June 2012, pg. 19, http://www.Federalreserve.gov/pubs/bulletin/2012/pdf/scf12.pdf (Last viewed 8/23/2012).

the marketplace, brings their concerns to the attention of companies, and assists in addressing their complaints.

Top consumer complaints

The CFPB's Office of Consumer Response used a phased approach to the roll-out of complaint handling by product. In FY 2013, Consumer Response added the ability to handle complaints about credit reporting, money transfers, and debt collection.

Consumer Response handled approximately 144,000 consumer complaints about credit cards, mortgages, student loans, bank accounts or services, vehicle and consumer loans, credit reporting, debt collection, and money transfers in FY 2013.

TABLE 20: Top consumer complaints in FY 2013[10]

Complaint category	Approximate number of complaints
Mortgage	63,100
Credit card	17,100
Bank accounts and services	18,100
Credit reporting	20,900
Debt collection	13,900
Private student loan	4,100
Consumer loan	4,900
Money transfer	550
Other	1,500

10 Consumer Financial Protection Bureau Consumer Complaint Database.

TABLE 21: Top 3 issues for top 5 products in FY 2013

Issue type	Number of complaints
Mortgage	
Loan modification, collection, foreclosure	37,700
Loan servicing, payments, escrow account	14,600
Settlement process and costs	2,300
Credit card	
Billing disputes	3,100
APR or interest rate	1,200
Identity theft / Fraud / Embezzlement	1,100
Bank accounts and services	
Account opening, closing, or management	7,800
Deposits and withdrawals	4,600
Problems caused by my funds being low	2,500
Credit reporting	
Credit reporting company's investigation	2,400
Incorrect information on credit report	15,100
Unable to get credit report/credit score	1,900
Debt collection	
Continued attempts to collect debt not owed	4,400
Communication tactics	3,000
Taking/threatening an illegal action	1,700

This outcome will be accomplished through the following strategies and investments:

Strategies

- Collect, analyze, and leverage Consumer Response operational data to enable continuous improvement of our services to consumers.

- Develop a seamless approach to delivery of appropriate and useful Consumer Response data within the CFPB and to the public so that information is timely, understandable, and maintains consumer privacy.

- Automate key internal operational systems, particularly the intake and routing process, in order to effectively scale Consumer Response operations.

- Maintain a robust training and development program to support Consumer Response operations as volume and product coverage increase.

Investments

PERSONNEL

Hire additional staff to support intake, investigations, and data analysis in order to review, route, and address consumer complaints.

CONSUMER RESPONSE SYSTEM AND CONTACT CENTER SUPPORT

Make system investments in order to support the expansion of complaint handling to new products, improve the ease of use of the consumer and company portals, develop a scalable, risk-based approach to addressing consumer complaints, and make complaint data available to stakeholders through additional portals and to the public.

CONSUMER RESPONSE OPERATIONAL AND PROGRAM SUPPORT

Assist ongoing internal work to execute and refine its operations strategy, focusing on operational support, performance management support, and performance improvement services.

OPTIMIZING CFPB COMMUNICATION AND CONSUMER ENGAGEMENT CHANNELS

Assess the use of various communication channels offered by the CFPB and improve the users' experience according to the consumers' needs, whether related to submitting a complaint, accessing CFPB data, or learning about managing important financial decisions.

CONSUMER RESPONSE SYSTEM–NATURAL LANGUAGE PROCESSING

Gain greater efficiency and effectiveness in complaint handling to respond to the anticipated increase of interactions with consumers as the Bureau adds to the number of available services and these services become better known to the public.

We will assess our progress through the following three performance goals:

Performance goal 2.1.1: Decrease time between receiving and closing a complaint.

Facilitate efficient handling of a consumer complaint throughout the complaint process – from when the CFPB receives a complaint through when the CFPB completes an investigation, if applicable

1. **Intake Cycle Time:** Ensure complaints are routed to companies for response in a timely manner

2. **Company Cycle Time:** Ensure companies provide timely responses to consumer complaints

3. **Consumer Cycle Time:** Ensure consumers have adequate time to review company responses

4. **Investigations Cycle Time:** Ensure investigations are completed in a timely manner

PERFORMANCE MEASURE

TABLE 22: Intake cycle time

	FY 2012	FY 2013	FY 2014	FY 2015
Target	NA	3 days	3 days	2 days
Actual	7 days	1 day	NA	NA

TABLE 23: Company cycle time

	FY 2012	FY 2013	FY 2014	FY 2015
Target	NA	15 days	15 days	15 days
Actual	14 days	12 days	NA	NA

TABLE 24: Consumer cycle time

	FY 2012	FY 2013	FY 2014	FY 2015
Target	NA	30 days	30 days	30 days
Actual	16 days	4 days	NA	NA

TABLE 25: Investigation cycle time

	FY 2012	FY 2013	FY 2014	FY 2015
Target	NA	45 days	45 days	NA
Actual	78 days	78 days	NA	NA

PROGRESS UPDATE AND FUTURE ACTION

Complaint volume almost doubled from 74,000 complaints in FY 2012 to 144,000 in FY 2013. In addition, Consumer Response added the ability to accept credit reporting, money transfer, and debt collection complaints during FY 2013. Consumer Response refined its complaint handling processes and systems, increasing efficiencies through automation where possible, for example, to address the increased complaint volume and complexity and to improve its overall complaint handling operation. Process and system changes implemented in the investigations part of the complaint lifecycle, as well as product-specific training in FY 2013 are expected to reduce the Investigations Cycle Time in FY 2014.

Performance goal 2.1.2: Facilitate the timely response to consumer complaints by companies.

The CFPB facilitates timely response to consumer complaints by using a dedicated company portal to route complaints to companies for response. Once routed, complaints appear in real time in company portals where companies can review and respond to the complaint, triggering communications to consumers about the company's response to their complaints.

PERFORMANCE MEASURE

TABLE 26: The percentage of complaints routed through the company portal

	FY 2012	FY 2013	FY 2014	FY 2015
Target	NA	85%	87%	89%
Actual	83%	87%	NA	NA

PROGRESS UPDATE AND FUTURE ACTION

In FY 2013, the CFPB introduced a web form for companies to sign up for the company portal and established portal access and trained staff of approximately 1,600 companies to respond to complaints on the portal. In FY 2014, the Bureau will continue its work related to the launch of additional complaint handling by product and service.

Performance goal 2.1.3: Expand capacity to handle consumer complaints.

Consumer complaints shed light on the challenges consumers face in obtaining financial products and services and inform the CFPB's efforts to make consumer financial markets work better and empower consumers to live better financial lives.

PERFORMANCE MEASURE

TABLE 27: Number of consumer complaints handled

	FY 2012	FY 2013	FY 2014	FY 2015
Target	NA	125,000	200,000	225,000
Actual	74,000	144,000	NA	NA

PROGRESS UPDATE AND FUTURE ACTION

In FY 2013, the Bureau expanded the products and services about which it accepts complaints beyond credit cards, mortgages, bank accounts and services, consumer loans, and private student loan to include money transfers, credit reporting, and debt collection complaints. In FY 2014, the CFPB began to accept complaints about payday loans and plans to expand to accept other products and services under its authority.

The Bureau also expanded its Consumer Complaint Database, which started with credit cards in June 2012, to include complaints about additional products. In March 2013, the Bureau added complaints about mortgages, bank account and services, private student loans, and other consumer loan complaints to the database, as well as adding a sub-product field. In May 2013, the Bureau added credit reporting and money transfer complaints as well as fields for sub-issue and state. In November 2013, debt collection complaints were added to the database.

Outcome 2.2: *Help consumers understand the costs, risks, and tradeoffs of financial decisions; build trusted relationships that are interactive and informative to help consumers take control of their financial choices to meet their own goals; and raise effectiveness of those who provide financial education services to increase financial literacy.*

Outcome leader: Associate Director, Consumer Education and Engagement

The CFPB works to provide consumers with the information, knowledge, and financial education needed in order to make well-informed decisions. The Bureau also works to enhance the financial knowledge and capability of the country as a whole. In addition to improving overall financial capability, the CFPB focuses on addressing the unique financial challenges faced by four specific populations.

Students

29 million Population enrolled in colleges and universities[11]

The benefits of higher education are well documented. Four-year college graduates experience a number of economic benefits over high school graduates, including higher median earnings and lower unemployment rates. Evidence indicates that these disparities are growing.[12] Demand for higher education and college financing are at all-time highs. Over the past decade, the size of the student loan market has been increasing steadily. At over $1.2 trillion in loans outstanding, the market for student loans is now the second largest component of household debt after mortgages.[13]

---

11 U.S. Department of Education, National Center for Education Statistics, Fall 2009 and Fall 2010, table prepared February 2012, http://nces.ed.gov/programs/digest/d11/tables/dt11_230.asp (Last viewed 8/23/2012).

12 College Board Advocacy and Policy Center, "Education Pays 2010 In Brief: The Benefits of Higher Education for Individuals and Society," 2010, http://trends.collegeboard.org/sites/default/files/brief/education-pays-2010-in-brief.pdf (Last viewed 2/14/2013).

13 The Department of Education and Consumer Financial Protection Bureau, "Private Student Loans Report," July 20, 2012, http://www.consumerfinance.gov/reports/private-student-loans-report/ (last viewed 9/10/12).

FIGURE 6: Average cost of attending school is increasing[14]

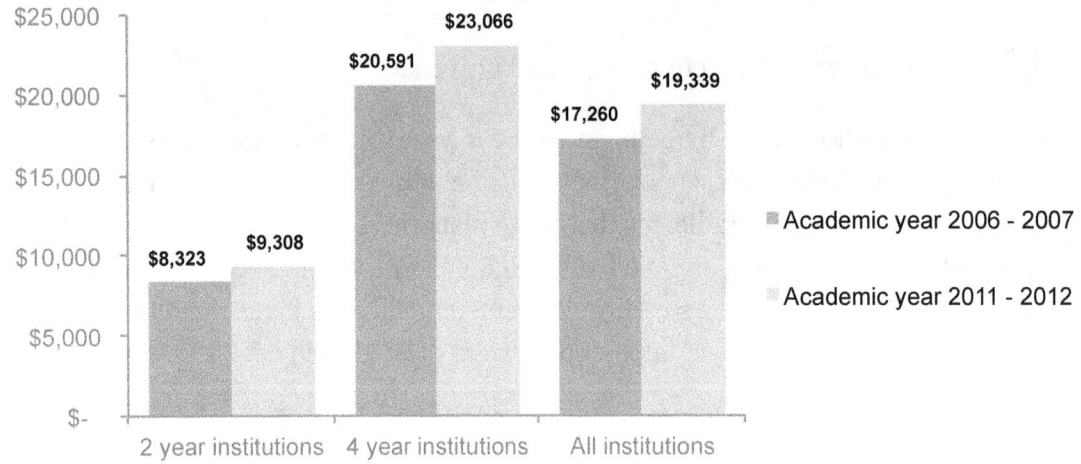

Over half of all students graduate with debt.[15]

- **57%** of students who earned bachelor's degrees in 2011-2012 from the public four-year university at which they began graduated with debt. Average debt per borrower was $22,000.

- **65%** of students who earned bachelor's degrees in 2011-2012 from the private nonprofit four-year colleges at which they began graduated with debt. Average debt per borrower was $28,000. Total balance of student debt outstanding is large and growing. Today, outstanding student debt is over $1 trillion[16] having tripled since 2003.[17]

---

14 U.S. Department of Education, National Center for Education Statistics, "Digest of Education Statistics 2010," table 345, http://nces.ed.gov/pubs2011/2011015.pdf (Last viewed 8/23/2012).

15 College Board Advocacy and Policy Center, "Trends in Student Aid" http://trends.collegeboard.org/student-aid/figures-tables/average-debt-levels-public-sector-bachelors-degree-recipients-over-time (Last viewed 12/13/2013).

16 The Department of Education and Consumer Financial Protection Bureau, "Private Student Loans Report," July 20, 2012, http://www.consumerfinance.gov/reports/private-student-loans-report/ (last viewed 9/12/2012).

17 Federal Reserve Bank of New York, "Quarterly Report on Household Debt and Credit," August 2012, pg. 3, http://www.newyorkfed.org/research/national_economy/householdcredit/DistrictReport_Q22012.pdf (last viewed 8/30/2012).

Older Americans

50 million Population age 62 and older[18]

Aging poses a number of unique financial challenges. Older Americans face complicated decisions about finances, retirement, and long-term planning. With the shift from defined-benefit to defined-contribution plans and other forms of "do-it-yourself retirement" such as IRAs making sound financial choices are especially important. According to the FINRA 2012 Financial Capability study, only 41% of non-retired respondents indicated that they had a self-directed retirement plan (a 401K or IRA).[19] Furthermore, Older Americans are frequently targeted for scams and financial exploitation. As people age some will experience a decline in their ability to handle finances putting them at risk of making poor decisions or increasing the risk that they will become victims of financial exploitation by scam artists or even by family members or legal fiduciaries.

> As we age, we face a number of complicated decisions related to finances, retirement, and long-term planning. Aging may impact one's ability to manage finances.
>
> - **22%** of Americans ages 71+ have mild cognitive impairment.[20]
>
> - **12%** of Americans ages 65+ have Alzheimer's disease.[21]
>
> This makes older Americans particularly susceptible to financial mistreatment and exploitation.
>
> - **5%** of Americans 60+ are victims of financial mistreatment by a family member.[22]

---

18 U.S. Census Bureau, "The Older Population in 2010," table 1, http://www.census.gov/population/age/data/2010.html (last viewed 2/14/2013).

19 Financial Capability in the United States, FINRA Investment Education Foundation, http://www.usfinancialcapability.org/downloads/NFCS_2012_Report_Natl_Findings.pdf.

20 B. L. Plassman et al., "Prevalence of Cognitive Impairment without Dementia in the United States," Archives of Internal Medicine 148, no. 6: 427–34.

21 Alzheimer's Association Study, "2011 Alzheimer's Disease Facts and Figures," 2011, http://www.alz.org/downloads/facts_figures_2011.pdf (last viewed 8/30/2012).

22 R. Acierno et al, "Prevalence and Correlates of Emotional, Physical, Sexual and Financial Abuse and Potential Neglect in the United States: The National Elder Mistreatment Study," American Journal of Public Health 100 no 2: 292-7.

Servicemembers

22 million Population (including veterans)[23]

The CFPB believes servicemembers should be able to accomplish their mission without worrying about illegal or harmful financial practices. Military life has challenges with powerful financial repercussions for uniformed military personnel, veterans, military retirees, and their families.

Servicemembers are an attractive target for both good and bad lenders.

- Servicemembers are required to pay their legitimate debts and can lose their security clearances over financial problems, so lenders are more confident they can collect their debts.

- Military families often start young, leading to big money management decisions by first-time decision makers.[24]

- Over **39%** of enlisted servicemembers are less than 25 years old. **52%** of the force is married. **43%** have two children.

Servicemembers face unique risks.

- Deployments, change of duty stations, and emergencies can lead to unplanned and unique financial challenges and leave servicemembers without adequate resources to resolve them.

- Loyalty to the service leads marketers to tie their pitches to the military, a strategy called "affinity marketing" that can cause servicemembers to overlook unfavorable aspects of the marketed products.

- Frequent relocation can mean household separation and other unforeseen expenses.

---

23 National Center for Veterans Analysis and Statistics "Veteran Population Projects; FY 2000 to FY 2036;" October 2010, http://www.va.gov/vetdata/docs/QuickFacts/population_quickfacts.pdf (last viewed 8/30/2012).

24 Office of the Deputy Under Secretary of Defense, "2012 Demographics: Profile of the Military Community," 11/26/2013 2011, http://www.defense.gov/home/features/2011/0111_initiative/ strengthening_our_military_january_2011.pdf (last viewed 8/30/2012).

Low-income and economically vulnerable

68 million adults are unbanked or underbanked.[25]

46.5 million live below the official poverty line.[26]

The CFPB focuses on identifying approaches that help this population achieve economic stability and works to ensure that the financial marketplace works for all consumers, including those who have been traditionally underserved.

Underbanked: an individual who has a checking or savings account and also used payday lending or certain other services from nonbanks.

Unbanked: an individual who does not have either a checking or savings account.

Economically vulnerable: low-income households, consumers with thin or no credit file, and households with limited savings. The CFPB focuses on approaches that enhance the financial capability of low-income and other economically vulnerable consumers.

Many Americans are or are at risk of becoming economically vulnerable.

- **34%** of Americans live on income below two times the poverty level (roughly $46,000 for a family of four).[27] **44%** of Americans have almost no savings and would fall into poverty after three months of job loss or illness that left them without an income.[28]

Lower income households are more likely to be underserved.

- **~20%** of households with income under $30,000 are unbanked.[29]

---

25 Federal Deposit Insurance Corporation, "2011 National Survey of Unbanked and Underbanked Households," 2012, http://economicinclusion.gov/surveys/2011household/.

26 US Census Bureau Income, Poverty, and Health Insurance Coverage in the United States: 2012.

27 U.S. Department of Commerce, "Income, Poverty, and Health Insurance Coverage in the United States: 2011," September 2012, pg. 18, table 5, http://www.census.gov/prod/2012pubs/p60-243.pdf (last viewed 2/14/2013).

28 U.S. Department of Commerce, "Income, Poverty, and Health Insurance Coverage in the United States: 2011," September 2012, pg. 18, table 5, http://www.census.gov/prod/2012pubs/p60-243.pdf (last viewed 2/14/2013).

29 Corporation for Enterprise Development, "2013 Asset and Opportunity Scorecard,"http://scorecard.assetsandopportunity.org/2013/measure/liquid-asset-poverty-rate (last viewed 8/29/2012).

This outcome will be accomplished through the following strategies and investments:

Strategies

- Provide tools and information to the public to help individuals make decisions about money that will serve their own life goals through delivery by both the CFPB and other trusted intermediaries.

- Analyze consumer financial experiences to help shape policy and influence product change to make the financial environment safer and more beneficial for consumers.

- Collaborate with third parties to encourage the development of effective financial skills and habits by adding in financial capability training to other types of social service programs.

- Strengthening the impact and effectiveness of K-12 and adult financial education by fostering take-up of best practices; facilitating partnerships; and identifying and seeking to fill gaps.

Investments

PERSONNEL

Hire additional staff to support financial education, consumer engagement, outreach, policy, and research activities.

CONSUMER EXPERIENCE PROGRAM

Enable the CFPB to continue to research, design, develop, launch, and continually optimize the premier consumer-facing products available through consumerfinance.gov, and execute marketing and editorial strategies to increase awareness of and engagement with these products. The Consumer Experience Program is a platform for building a trusted relationship with the American public by offering a series of modules that provide actionable advice to consumers navigating the most difficult and significant financial decisions they face in the marketplace, including paying for college, owning a home, and making retirement-related decisions.

CONSUMER EDUCATION CAMPAIGNS

Continue to develop consumer education campaigns on specific topics that may include print and broadcast media outreach, videos, and low-cost, targeted information to communicate financial education information to a diverse range of audiences. The topics and approaches of the educational campaigns will vary, but may include remittances and the delivery of financial education through libraries.

UNDERSERVED AND SPECIAL POPULATIONS PROGRAM

Pilot projects for improving financial decision making for underserved and special populations, including youth, low-income Americans, older Americans, and other specific populations.

UNDERSERVED AND SPECIAL POPULATIONS OUTREACH

Continue to develop and distribute financial education and empowerment information for various populations including servicemembers, students, older Americans, low income Americans, Americans with disabilities, and other specific underserved populations. These materials are often delivered through intermediaries that provide unique access to consumers and communities that have unique financial education and empowerment needs.

OPTIMIZING CFPB COMMUNICATION AND CONSUMER ENGAGEMENT CHANNELS

Assess the experience of various communication channels offered by CFPB, especially in support of improving the consumer's financial education and ability to manage important financial decisions.

YOUR MONEY, YOUR GOALS

The agency recently launched the *Your Money, Your Goals* program, which is used by social services staff to help clients manage their finances by identifying financial goals, creating savings plans and managing debt. We are conducting a field test of the financial empowerment toolkit for social services staff that equips them to "have the money talk" in ways that work within their service delivery model. Following the field test, the toolkit will be revised and subsequently launched nationally during 2014.

We will assess our progress through the following three performance goals:

Performance goal 2.2.1: Significantly increase targeted outreach activities and digital education materials and research in order to engage consumers at the right moment.

The CFPB works to arm consumers with the knowledge, tools, and capabilities they need in order to make better informed financial decisions by engaging them in the right moments of their financial lives, when the consumer is most receptive to seeking out and acting on assistance. To that end, the CFPB offers and is developing a variety of tools, programs, and initiatives that provide targeted, meaningful, and accessible assistance and information to consumers around life moments that correspond to major financial choices.

PERFORMANCE MEASURE

TABLE 28: Targeted populations or organizations directly serving targeted populations reached by digital content, decision tools, educational materials and resources.[30]

	FY 2012	FY 2013	FY 2014	FY 2015
Target	NA	808,114	2,100,000	2,500,000
Actual	404,057	1,903,417	NA	NA

PROGRESS UPDATE AND FUTURE ACTION

In FY 2013, the CFPB continued to serve consumers with just-in-time financial information through Ask CFPB, an online database of consumers' common questions around financial products and services. The CFPB launched a major release of Paying for College, an online suite of information and tools for helping consumers understand their after-graduation monthly debt payments before choosing a financial aid package. Additionally, the CFPB launched a Spanish-language website that includes information on how to submit a complaint in Spanish and Ask CFPB questions and answers.

In FY 2014, the CFPB will also make improvements to its existing Paying for College product, alongside marketing investments that will maximize the awareness and value of the product for consumers. In addition, the CFPB will launch a fully-integrated campaign to educate the public about changes in the mortgage market, culminating in the launch of Owning a Home, a consumer experience module. The module will help consumers successfully navigate the mortgage shopping experience and comparison shop.

In FY 2015, the CFPB will continue improving its existing suite of consumer experience products, and expand it to cover consumers' key decisions about retirement. The CFPB will present a more seamless, unified experience to consumers across Ask CFPB, Tell Your Story, and complaint intake. All of this work will be supported by the implementation of an enterprise

---

30 The actuals and targets above represent unique web visitors only. As the CFPB expands data collection capabilities on outreach activities, additional content will be included in this measure.

marketing strategy that drives awareness and maximizes the reach and impact of the CFPB's tools and information.

Performance goal 2.2.2: Improve the understanding of successful financial decision-making approaches by identifying key success factors in financial health.

The CFPB believes that financial education's primary goal is to help consumers take the steps necessary to make choices that will improve their financial well-being. However, very little empirical research has been conducted regarding what variables measure financial health in terms of real-world outcomes for consumers. By defining these variables through data-driven research, the Bureau will be able to define what knowledge and skills are associated with financial health. This research will inform the Bureau's ongoing efforts to identify, highlight, and spread effective approaches to financial education.

PERFORMANCE MEASURE

Tools created to identify key success factors in financial education.

Targets

FY 2013: Identify variables that are likely to be key drivers of financial health
FY 2014: Develop and test metrics (questions) that accurately measure those variables
FY 2015: Develop and implement framework for integration into Consumer Education and Engagement programs and activities

Actuals

FY 2012: Contract awarded for research and development project to identify variables and develop metrics
FY 2013: We identified the variables that are likely to be key drivers of financial health.

PROGRESS UPDATE AND FUTURE ACTION

The Bureau's work towards the performance goal is on track, with expected deliverables and interim targets being met according to the anticipated project timeline.

In FY 2013, the Bureau conducted a broad array of research to identify what specific knowledge, behavior, and personal traits are likely to predict financial well-being for American consumers. This included a thorough formal review of the most relevant research literature; designing, completing and analyzing extended one-on-one interviews with a socioeconomically and geographically broad sample of working-age and older Americans and professional financial practitioners; and soliciting and collecting collaborative input and peer discussion from academic, policy, and practicing experts. Based on this, the CFPB has developed a preliminary, first-of-its-kind, comprehensive definition of financial well-being that speaks to the goals and perspectives of consumers, as well as a set of specific variables that are likely to be key drivers of financial well-being.

In FY 2014, the CFPB will rigorously develop and test metrics (measurement tools) that accurately measure financial well-being and related variables. These measurement tools will allow the CFPB and others to more accurately assess consumer financial health, target educational efforts, test hypotheses about key drivers of financial health, and assess the effectiveness of different approaches to improving consumer financial well-being. The CFPB will then promote the most effective approaches that support better outcomes for consumers.

Once the research is complete, the CFPB's Division of Consumer Education and Engagement will develop and implement a framework to integrate this project's findings and new measurement tools into other consumer education and engagement initiatives. This will likely include our research projects, direct-to-consumer resources, and recommendations for intermediaries to promote effective approaches to the financial education field. This effort is detailed under "Underserved and Special Populations Research" in the Investments section of Outcome 3.2.

Performance goal 2.2.3: Promote fair lending compliance and education by leading and participating in fair lending outreach activities.

As one of its core functions, the Office of Fair Lending is responsible for "working with private industry, fair lending, civil rights, [and] consumer and community advocates on the promotion of fair lending compliance and education." (Dodd-Frank Act, Section 1013(c)(2)(c).) CFPB conducts fair lending outreach activities through numerous channels, such as issuing compliance bulletins targeted to industry; delivering speeches and presentations on fair lending and access to credit matters to industry, consumer and community groups, and others; and participating in smaller meetings and discussions with external stakeholders.

PERFORMANCE MEASURE

TABLE 29: Number of outreach activities on fair lending and access to credit

	FY 2012	FY 2013	FY 2014	FY 2015
Target	NA	55	35	35
Actual	51	56	NA	NA

PERFORMANCE GOAL UPDATE AND FUTURE ACTION

In FY 2013, the Office of Fair Lending and Equal Opportunity executed against its mission to promote fair, equitable, and nondiscriminatory access to credit for individuals and communities by participating in 56 fair lending outreach activities.

Through numerous speeches, panel remarks, presentations, and smaller discussions on fair lending matters, the Bureau reached out to various important stakeholders, including congressional committee staff, industry leaders and participants, national and state fair lending and fair housing groups, community advocates, and consumer advocates. These engagements allowed the Bureau both to explain existing and emerging fair lending issues and risks to external stakeholders and to inform the Bureau's fair lending oversight work.

The Bureau issued a bulletin on compliance in indirect auto lending (CFPB Bulletin 2013-02) and prepared for release a bulletin on HMDA compliance management and resubmission (CFPB Bulletin 2013-11) to help increase transparency around our supervisory process in both mortgage and auto lending and to provide guidance to industry actors on effective fair lending compliance.

Going forward, the Bureau will continue to champion fair and equal access to credit through outreach activities, and plans on pursuing an even more concentrated approach. The Bureau will be conducting fewer and more strategically focused activities on fair lending, and has adjusted the targets for FY 2014 and FY 2015 to reflect this strategic approach in fair lending outreach.

Goal 3

Inform the public, policy makers, and the CFPB's own policymaking with data-driven analysis of consumer finance markets and consumer behavior.

Understanding how consumer financial markets work, the avenues for innovation in financial products and services, and the potential for risk to consumers is a core component of the CFPB's mission. The CFPB's aim is to ground all of its work—from writing rules and litigating enforcement actions to its outreach and financial literacy efforts—in the realities of the marketplace and the complexities of consumer behavior.

This requires use of data, strong partnerships within the CFPB and externally to ensure that we continue to monitor markets effectively, technology tools, and employees with the skills and capabilities needed to analyze data and distill insights.

The CFPB's research will support building an understanding of the markets we regulate and the nature of consumer behavior in these markets. It will also support the consideration of the potential benefits and costs of the CFPB's work to consumers and institutions, including effects on access by consumers to consumer financial products or services.

In all of the data used for its analyses, the Bureau will work to ensure that strong protections are in place around personally identifiable information. The Bureau will generally obtain datasets in a format such that no information is directly identifiable, and research/analysis products resulting from such data will use similarly de-identified information. The Bureau treats the information collected from participating persons and institutions consistently with our confidentiality regulations and all data and analyses are subject to legal and privacy review prior to their release.

TABLE 30: Budget by program, goal 3

Goal 3	FY 2013	FY 2014	FY 2015
Office of the Director	$1,308,676	$1,128,996	$1,177,931
Consumer Education, and Engagement	$5,285,542	$8,533,404	$9,871,720
Research, Markets, and Regulation	$23,712,486	$31,987,401	$28,810,208
Legal	$1,030,864	$1,511,124	$1,689,424
External Affairs	$725,095	$1,036,499	$1,171,143
Other Programs	$174,092	$431,463	$479,673
Centralized Services	$26,284,459	$13,808,109	$12,822,081
Total	**$58,521,214**	**$58,436,996**	**$56,022,179**

The CFPB will accomplish its third goal by achieving two outcomes

Outcome 3.1: *Monitor markets and conduct research to surface financial trends and emergent risks relevant to consumers.*

Outcome leader: Associate Director, Research, Markets and Regulations

This outcome will be accomplished through the following strategies and investments:

Strategies

- Acquire, collect, and maintain the data necessary to properly monitor select markets for emerging risks and positive innovations.

- Coordinate with other Federal agencies, including the Office of Financial Research, to ensure the most efficient use of data and avoid duplication.

- Build and maintain technological infrastructure required to support market intelligence through the integration of diverse internal and external data.

Investments

PERSONNEL

Hire additional experts in particular industries, as well as additional economists and other researchers.

CREDIT CARD DATABASE

Maintain a credit card database, including both summary and de-identified loan-level data, covering approximately 80% of the credit card marketplace. This investment will allow the Bureau to conduct empirically sound research essential to informing data-driven decisions throughout Bureau activities.

MORTGAGE DATABASE

Develop and maintain databases that will provide the Bureau with a representative view of the mortgage market, demonstrating up to 95% of the market.

EVIDENCE-BASED CONSUMER FINANCIAL MARKET RESEARCH

Conduct evidence-based research to build foundational knowledge in financial trends and emergent risks relevant to consumers.

OTHER MARKET DATA

Acquire and maintain various commercially available market datasets in order to support research and regulations activities.

HMDA DEVELOPMENT AND IMPLEMENTATION

Support a concept-of-operations study and development of future-state functional requirements in consideration of a potential redesign of the current HMDA framework.

We will access our progress through the following performance goal:

Performance goal 3.1.1: Monitor the credit card and mortgage markets through data.

The credit card and mortgage markets are both critical to consumers. Having quantitative data on both markets makes it easier for the Bureau to monitor trends and implications for both consumers and providers. These data also strengthen the evidentiary basis for Bureau policy-making.

PERFORMANCE MEASURE

TABLE 31: Percentage of the credit card market monitored through data

	FY 2012	FY 2013	FY 2014	FY 2015
Target	NA	80%	80%	80%
Actual	77%	85%	NA	NA

TABLE 32: Percentage of the mortgage origination and servicing markets monitored through data

	FY 2012	FY 2013	FY 2014	FY 2015
Target	NA	95%	95%	95%
Actual	95%	90%	NA	NA

PROGRESS UPDATE AND FUTURE ACTION

The reported Actual FY 2013 level of performance for data coverage of the mortgage market is 90%, which is lower than the reported FY 2012 coverage of 95%. In FY 2012, the CFPB was able to combine data from HMDA with the data from Nationwide Mortgage Licensing System & Registry (NMLS) (and some other sources) to create an aggregate picture of 95% of the market. This match has not yet been completed in FY 2013, and as a result, the Bureau reports the 90% figure for FY 2013 based primarily on the HMDA data. Importantly, the CFPB has the NMLS data and other data as well: however, without doing the necessary matches and analysis, we chose to report the HMDA-based estimate alone. Going forward, the Bureau plans to apply a standard method for assessing data coverage of the mortgage market.

Through the maintenance of the CFPB Credit Card Database, the Bureau is able to cover a sizable portion of the cards market with de-identified loan-level detail. The Bureau uses publicly available resources (HMDA, NMLS, call reports) for monitoring the mortgage markets, and supplements these sources with two commercial services for data regarding originations and servicing. CoreLogic provides servicing data on loans serviced by the largest servicers in the US (just over 53% of outstanding mortgages) and BlackBox LLC provides data on loans extant in private label securities.

In FY 2013, the CFPB began a partnership with the Federal Housing Finance Agency (FHFA) to build the National Mortgage Database (NMDB). This work continues in FY 2014. For this database, the FHFA and the Bureau have procured (from a credit reporting agency) credit information with respect to a random and representative sample of 5% of mortgages held by consumers. The NMDB is the first dataset that will provide a truly representative sample of mortgages so as to allow analysis of mortgages over the life of the loans, including firsts, seconds, and home equity loans.

In all of the data used for its analyses, the Bureau will work to ensure that strong protections are in place around personally identifiable information. The Bureau will generally obtain datasets in a format such that no information is directly identifiable and research/analysis products resulting from such data will use similarly de-identified information. The Bureau treats the information collected from participating persons and institutions consistently with our confidentiality regulations and all data and analyses are subject to legal and privacy review.

Outcome 3.2: *Articulate a research-driven, evidence-based perspective on consumer financial markets, consumer behavior, and regulations to inform the public discourse, inform Bureau thinking on priority areas, identify areas where Bureau intervention may improve market outcomes, and support efforts to reduce outdated, unnecessary, or unduly burdensome regulations.*

Outcome leader: Associate Director, Research, Markets, and Regulations

This outcome will be accomplished through the following strategies and investments:

Strategies

- Collect and analyze data in order to improve understanding, regulation, and functioning of consumer financial markets and behavior.

- Help to make the market work better for special populations such as students, older Americans, servicemembers and veterans, and low-income and economically vulnerable consumers through selected policy work.

- Institutionalize cross-Bureau collaboration to ensure our work is informed by the CFPB's internal research and expertise.

- Develop and maintain the tools and technology required to effectively, efficiently, and securely disseminate data and research for internal and external audiences.

Investments

PERSONNEL

Expand research capacity in order to achieve Bureau-wide priorities.

COMPLIANCE COST STUDY

Study the costs of compliance related to existing and new consumer regulations to improve the Bureau's capacity to write effective rules and ease compliance burden.

FINANCIAL EDUCATION RESEARCH

Develop and test metrics that effectively measure relevant consumer financial knowledge, behavior, and well-being. The results of these studies will help the CFPB, other Financial Literacy and Education Commission agencies, and the broader financial education field to develop and support policies and programs that lead to better financial outcomes, skills, and habits for American consumers.

UNDERSERVED AND SPECIAL POPULATIONS RESEARCH

Identify unique factors that influence financial capabilities for youth, low-income Americans, older Americans, and other underserved populations, as well as evidence-based practices for effective financial education and empowerment. Related pilot programs will advance the understanding of interventions that can optimize financial decision-making.

CONSUMER EXPERIENCE PROGRAM

Enable the CFPB to research and continue optimizing the effectiveness of the Consumer Experience Program, a series of digital media modules that proved actionable advice to consumers navigating the most difficult financial decisions they face in the marketplace.

FINANCIAL EDUCATION INNOVATIONS

Design, develop, and arrange for testing of strategies to improve consumer financial decision-making.

EVIDENCE-BASED CONSUMER FINANCIAL MARKET RESEARCH

Conduct evidence-based research to inform policy-making and build foundational knowledge about how consumers make financial decisions

KNOW BEFORE YOU OWE–MORTGAGE CLOSING

Establish a dialogue and pilot tests regarding the stack of documentation associated with closing and potential innovations in the market that might create a more educational and empowering process for consumers.

FINANCIAL EDUCATION METRICS

Conduct research to determine how to measure financial well-being and identify the knowledge, skills, and habits associated with financially capable consumers. The Bureau will develop and test metrics that effectively measure relevant consumer financial knowledge, behavior, and well-being. The results of this study will help the CFPB, other Financial Literacy and Education Commission agencies, and the broader financial education field to develop and support policies and programs that lead to better financial outcomes, skills, and habits for American consumers. This is a continuation of the financial education metrics project which began in FY 2013. In FY 2014, the financial education metrics project will extend its findings from adult financial well-being research (metrics project) to children and youth and advance the findings from the quantitative testing of the financial well-being metrics developed for working adults.

We will access our progress through the following performance goal:

Performance goal 3.2.1: Increase the number of reports produced about specific consumer financial products, markets, or regulations and on consumer decision-making.

The Bureau conducts qualitative and quantitative research to deepen understanding of consumer decision making; consumer financial products and markets; and the effects of consumer financial regulations and policies. Periodically, the Bureau publishes reports of its research.

Bureau and independent research are intended to provide the Bureau and other policy makers with a stronger evidentiary foundation for policymaking. They are also intended to inform the public and enhance the public's participation in policymaking.

PERFORMANCE MEASURE

TABLE 33: Reports produced about specific consumer financial products, markets, or regulations and on consumer decision-making

	FY 2012	FY 2013	FY 2014	FY 2015
Target	4	5	5	5
Actual	2	4	NA	NA

PROGRESS UPDATE AND FUTURE ACTION

Preparing reports is central to the Bureau's commitment to evidence-based policy-making. The Bureau issued four prominent reports in FY 2013. These reports are intended to deepen the public's understanding of these issues and provide the Bureau and other policy makers with a stronger factual foundation on which to make policy judgments. The Bureau's Research, Markets and Regulations Division released the following notable public reports in FY 2013:

- *Analysis of Differences between Consumer- and Creditor-Purchased Credit Scores*

- *Key Dimensions and Processes in the U.S. Credit Reporting System: A review of how the nation's largest credit bureaus manage consumer data*

- *Payday Loans and Deposit Advance Products: A White Paper of Initial Data Findings*

- *CFPB Study of Overdraft Programs: A white paper of initial data findings*

In addition to these four reports released by the Bureau's Research, Markets and Regulations Division, the Bureau's Consumer Engagement and Education division released the following notable public reports in FY 2013:

- *Senior Designations for Financial Advisors: Reducing Consumer Confusion and Risks*

- *Navigating the Market: A comparison of spending on financial education and financial marketing*

In the future, the Bureau will include Consumer Engagement and Education's reports in the actuals and targets for this Performance measure. The Bureau has information gathering and other data analysis underway that will yield public reports in FY 2014. These research areas include: a study of the CARD Act; a study of compliance costs as related to the Bureau's deposit-related regulations; a review and examination of pre-dispute arbitration clauses and their effects on consumers; and other planned topics. With two of the above reports already released by November 2013, we are on schedule to meet the FY 2014 goal of publishing at least five reports.

Goal 4

Advance the CFPB's performance by maximizing resource productivity and enhancing impact.

In order to maximize the effectiveness of the consumer protections established by Federal consumer financial law, the CFPB must acquire, maintain, support, and direct its resources in a way that enables it to operate efficiently, effectively, and transparently. This means developing, maintaining, and continuously improving the policies and controls in place to ensure the CFPB has the resources it needs and puts those resources to the best use possible.

A key mission of the CFPB is to make financial products and services more transparent in the consumer marketplace. The CFPB will strive to achieve the same level of commitment to transparency in its own activities, while respecting consumer privacy and confidentiality. To accomplish this, the CFPB will develop and implement mechanisms and provide channels to maintain an open, collaborative dialogue with the public.

TABLE 34: Budget by program, goal 4

Goal 4	FY 2013	FY 2014	FY 2015
Office of the Director	$1,308,676	$1,128,996	$1,177,931
Operations	$54,171,404	$68,684,285	$69,744,184
Legal	$4,845,062	$6,761,617	$7,171,196
External Affairs	$2,658,680	$3,800,496	$4,294,192
Other Programs	$412,830	$992,961	$1,003,803
Centralized Services	$73,499,876	$40,162,723	$35,124,640
Total	$136,896,529	$121,531,078	$118,515,946

Outcome 4.1: *Attract, engage, and deploy a diverse workforce that meets dynamic challenges and provides effective oversight of the consumer financial marketplace.*

Outcome leader: Associate Director, Operations

The CFPB continues to pursue a strategic imperative to recruit and hire highly qualified individuals, focusing on filling vacancies at its headquarters in Washington, DC, and in its examiner workforce distributed across the country. To do so, the CFPB continued to identify and adopt best practices from the private and public sectors to hire, train and develop a diverse world-class workforce with the knowledge, skills and abilities required to effectively achieve our mission.

As we continue to work towards full capacity over the next couple of years, we are also placing an increased emphasis on the development and retention of those highly qualified individuals now on staff. This expanded focus will allow improvement efforts targeting the employee experience, development, retention and engagement.

This outcome will be accomplished by the following strategies and investments:

Strategies

- Recruit and retain a high-quality, diverse staff through effective workforce planning and talent acquisition methods, strong engagement, a comprehensive diversity and inclusion program, and a competitive compensation and benefits package.

- Create and sustain a high-performing workforce through innovative workforce learning, development and performance-management programs.

- Develop human capital infrastructure by creating human capital policies, improving human capital information systems, effectively allocating and prioritizing resources, and using mutual accountabilities to achieve desired human capital outcomes.

Investments

PERSONNEL

Continue to build capacity across the Bureau by hiring high-performing, diverse employees.

HUMAN CAPITAL SHARED-SERVICES, INFRASTRUCTURE, AND OPERATIONS

Contract with the Department of the Treasury to provide a variety of services, including pay and leave administration support, employee benefits administration and support, and human capital help desk and reporting support for timekeeping, personnel documentation, and performance management systems.

LEARNING, LEADERSHIP, AND ORGANIZATION DEVELOPMENT FACILITATION AND DESIGN

Support the development of high-quality learning solutions including core competency training, consumer financial market overview, new supervisor training, leadership training, diversity and inclusion training, and manager skill-building through coaching and organization development services. Support the improvement of organizational and group effectiveness through organizational interventions, workforce planning, and group or team action planning support.

OUTREACH, CANDIDATE RECRUITING, AND CANDIDATE SELECTION SUPPORT

Invest in candidate outreach, sourcing, recruiting, and selection support services to reach, attract, and hire high-performing, diverse staff. Invest in services such as print and social media, strategic, tailored candidate assessment methods to improve decision-making. Build and maintain strategic partnerships with colleges, universities, professional organizations, and affinity groups that serve diverse populations.

We will assess our progress through the following two performance goals:

Performance Goal 4.1.1: Recruit and retain high-performing, diverse employees with the right skills and abilities to meet mission driven goals and objectives.

A wide array of skills and abilities, which represent diversity and organizational makeup, is required for success in achieving our mission. We assess progress and performance on this goal by measuring employee perceptions of 1) the technical competence of the workforce and 2) diversity and inclusiveness. Strategies to improve in these areas target organizational effectiveness, workforce planning, diversity and inclusiveness interventions at the group and organizational levels.

PERFORMANCE MEASURE

TABLE 35: Annual Employee Survey (AES) rating on perceptions of technical competence of the CFPB staff (% favorable)[31]

	FY 2012	FY 2013	FY 2014	FY 2015
Target	NA	68.5%	68.5%	68.5%
Actual	65%	67%	NA	NA

PERFORMANCE MEASURE

TABLE 36: Annual Employee Survey rating on perceptions of workplace diversity and inclusiveness of the CFPB staff (% favorable)[32]

	FY 2012	FY 2013	FY 2014	FY 2015
Target	NA	76%	76%	76%
Actual	74.8%	76%	NA	NA

PROGRESS UPDATE AND FUTURE ACTION

In FY 2013, the Bureau recruited and hired talented employees, growing from 970 employees at the beginning of FY 2013 to 1,355 at fiscal year's end. The Offices of Human Capital, Minority and Women Inclusion (OMWI), and Equal Employment Opportunity (EEO) collaborated to develop targeted recruiting strategies and enhance workplace diversity. Strategies applied in FY 2013 that significantly expanded FY 2012 activity, include: partnering with affiliate organizations[33] to reach qualified diverse professionals; recruiting at nearly 30 minority-focused career events, and using internships to reinforce our diverse talent pipeline. As of the end of FY 2013, there were 24 interns on staff, 15 recent graduates, and 15 Presidential Management Fellows, including those employees continuing on Pathways appointments after conversion from other student programs. The Bureau also expanded the use of enhanced candidate assessment tools to support hiring into more than 70 different jobs at all levels of the organization and

---

31 The technical competence composite is comprised of ratings on three items from the AES survey, including "the workforce has the job-relevant knowledge and skills necessary to accomplish organizational goals."

32 The workplace diversity and inclusiveness composite is comprised of ratings on two items from the AES survey, which are "managers/supervisors/team leaders work well with employees of different backgrounds." and "my supervisor supports my need to balance work and other life issues."

33 Affiliate organizations included: the National Black MBA Association, the League of United Latin American Citizens, and Association of Latino Professionals in Finance and Accounting.

enhanced the technical training and on the job learning supporting employees in a variety of positions. These efforts contributed to a notable improvement in employee satisfaction with training received for current positions. In the future, the CFPB will continue its efforts to recruit and retain highly qualified and diverse candidates for a vibrant workforce.

In the area of technical competence, the CFPB has demonstrated improvement from FY 2012 level. In FY 2014, the Office of Human Capital will continue to refine the set of items utilized to assess technical competence. In addition, interventions to define learning and development, core competencies, and career paths should have a positive impact on this metric.

Performance goal 4.1.2: Increase the level of employee engagement.

Engagement has been described as a state of passion and commitment to the organization's goals on the part of each employee, which leads to their willingness to invest discretionary effort to ensure success. In the case of the Bureau, maintaining the initial motivation and excitement of the new workforce is critical to our future success. Individual employees' perception of the level of employee engagement is one way to measure the Bureau's success engaging its employees.

PERFORMANCE MEASURE

TABLE 37: Annual Employee Survey Engagement composite rating (% favorable)[34]

	FY 2012	FY 2013	FY 2014	FY 2015
Target	NA	76.5%	76.5%	76.5%
Actual	74%	73%	NA	NA

PROGRESS UPDATE AND FUTURE ACTION

The CFPB continues to present employees with a wide range of opportunities to demonstrate personal commitment to the organization's mission and goals. Concurrently, the CFPB has further developed functions dedicated to monitoring and improving organizational performance metrics, including metrics related to workplace environment and employee engagement. The CFPB's Culture Team was reinvigorated under new leadership and the Bureau has started to

---

34 The employee engagement composite is comprised of ratings on nine items from the AES survey, such as "my work gives me a feeling of personal accomplishment" and "the work I do is important."

forge a strong partnership with the CFPB's recently elected chapter of the National Treasury Employees Union (NTEU).

The CFPB also initiated efforts to improve employee engagement within offices and Divisions. However, many of these efforts started in the second half of FY 2013, leaving insufficient time before the July AES for improvements to take hold. The CFPB anticipates more positive results in FY 2014 due to concerted action planning efforts.

In FY 2014, the CFPB continues to ensure that reporting of AES 2013 results at the Division and office levels takes place in a structured and consistent manner, further improving on successes achieved in FY 2012. The Bureau's Office of Human Capital works directly with leaders of all Divisions to initiate action planning based on AES 2013 findings. Division leaders will bear responsibility for delivering improvement efforts and reporting on progress.

Outcome 4.2: *Enable the innovative use of technology for the benefit of efficient internal processes and effective public engagement.*

Outcome leader: Associate Director, Operations

The CFPB is committed to staying on the leading edge of technology and leveraging its technological resources to provide significant business value with lower costs. From developing online products that help inform consumers to making critical data available internally and to the public, technology is and will continue to be core to the CFPB's accomplishing its mission.

This outcome will be accomplished through the following strategies and investments

Strategies

- Establish a secure, responsive and cost-effective technology infrastructure to enable a 21st century agency.

- Continue to build, develop and improve next-generation online tools that help consumers get answers to questions. make financial decisions, and confront difficult financial circumstances.

- Maintain a robust platform for the public to visualize and make use of data maintained by the Bureau, such as consumer complaint data.

- Create a suite of enterprise-wide technology capabilities that maximizes the efficiencies of resources and costs.

Investments

PERSONNEL

Hire additional staff to enable the organization's continued support of Bureau activities including managing, operating and safeguarding the IT systems that host and store the CFPB's data; designing, and developing tools to facilitate data-driven analysis and consumer education; and implementing a 21st century cloud-based infrastructure that serves as the foundation for innovative technology.

INFRASTRUCTURE

Facilitate the CFPB's infrastructure independence efforts by allowing for the migration of critical services to a flexible, scalable CFPB-managed infrastructure capable of sustaining the Bureau's future growth.

DESIGN AND SOFTWARE DEVELOPMENT SUPPORT

Continue to strengthen the Bureau's capacity to design, develop, implement and maintain new tools with enhanced capabilities, features and functionalities for a variety of business applications that support the Bureau's mission.

CYBERSECURITY

Continue to enhance a robust cybersecurity program that secures and safeguards communications, data, and IT resources through a combination of comprehensive policies, continuous monitoring, and leading technologies.

PORTFOLIO MANAGEMENT

Enhance the successful deployment of projects through the continued use of disciplined methodologies including project management and agile development and facilitate the development of the long-term technology strategy that guides future mission capabilities.

DATA INFRASTRUCTURE AND ANALYSIS

Continue to build and develop a data driven strategy that is deployed on a technology architecture with scalable capabilities that will allow the Bureau to use and manage data to conduct predictive analytics and aid in better decision making.

We will assess our progress through the following two performance goals:

Performance goal 4.2.1: Release new datasets to the public, where legally permissible and appropriate, to allow for innovative uses of the data by individuals, non-profit entities, and businesses for the benefit of consumers.

The public uses data released by the government to build tools and provide resources to consumers to help them make the best financial decisions. The CFPB wants to support a culture of information and transparency by releasing useful data to the public when doing so is legally permissible and appropriate.

PERFORMANCE MEASURE

TABLE 38: Provision of data to the public in legally permissible and appropriate instances[35]

	FY 2012	FY 2013	FY 2014	FY 2015
Target	NA	5	7	7
Actual	3	4	NA	NA

PROGRESS UPDATE AND FUTURE ACTION

In FY 2013, the CFPB released four datasets including the Consumer Complaint Database, the Credit Card Agreement Database, the College Credit Card agreements and the Survey of Credit Card Pricing Plans. Additionally, in September 2013, the CFPB provided access to the HMDA data via its website.

In January 2014, the CFPB will launch its public data platform where the HMDA data will be available for use by industry advocates and consumers to intuitively search and work with the data and conduct analysis. The CFPB plans to release two more large datasets in FY 2014. When releasing datasets, the Bureau protects certain data in the database from public disclosure, including personally-identifiable information, in accordance with applicable laws and regulations.

Performance goal 4.2.2: Improve the efficiency of internal processes and

---

35 Datasets are reported on a cumulative basis.

procedures.

Technology can help us improve the efficiency of the CFPB so that we serve more consumers in a better way.

PERFORMANCE MEASURE

Efficiency of internal processes and procedures

Targets

FY 2013:

1. Deploy a business intelligence tool

2. Deploy a business process automation platform and develop applications leveraging it

FY 2014:

1. Continue to build out core infrastructure services

FY 2015:

1. Operate and maintain core infrastructure services

2. Deploy mission capabilities to support Supervision and Enforcement activities

Actuals

FY 2012:

1. Launched AskCFPB

2. Launched an upgrade of the Intranet including an upgraded wiki, personnel directory, and internal news feed

3. Deployed a performance management system

FY 2013:

1. Development of Business Intelligence Tool

2. Debt Collection Product Launch

3. Paying for College

4. Infrastructure Independence Phase I

In FY 2013, the Bureau developed a business intelligence tool that provides a user-friendly platform for exploring and analyzing data. This platform will be implemented by the first quarter within FY 2014. During FY 2013, the Bureau initiated an effort to prioritize and manage the Bureau's information technology needs resulting in more streamlined and disciplined processes. The results of the prioritization efforts allowed for the successful deployment of over 50% of technology projects, including the Debt Collection and Paying for College product launches.

In FY 2014, the Bureau will continue the work to build out the core infrastructure capabilities and create a long term technology strategy that guides future mission capabilities.

Outcome 4.3: *Enable the operation of a high-performing organization by ensuring effective and efficient management, protection of CFPB resources, rigorous internal controls, and full compliance with the law.*

Outcome leader: Associate Director, Operations

The CFPB has the obligation to act as a good steward of public funds. The CFPB will monitor its operations and conduct periodic evaluations to ensure it maintains good financial practices and robust internal controls.

This outcome will be accomplished through the following strategies and investments:

Strategies

- Use data to supervise and coordinate all financial operations of the Bureau consistent with the requirements of laws and regulations.

- Develop a team of high-performing professionals with expertise in budget, financial management, procurement, internal controls and travel operations.

- Develop and maintain integrated accounting and financial management and travel systems in order to support the effective use of resources.

Investments

PERSONNEL

Hire additional staff to ensure resources continue to be used efficiently and effectively, and transparency and accountability are maintained.

AUDITS OF THE BUREAU

Continue to work with the Office of Inspector General (OIG) of the Board of Governors of the Federal Reserve System and the Bureau of Consumer Financial Protection, the Government Accountability Office (GAO), and an independent contractor for external auditing and oversight of the Bureau's operations and budget.

FINANCIAL MANAGEMENT SUPPORT SERVICES

Continue to provide financial management services in the areas of budget execution, purchasing, accounts payable, accounts receivable, and general ledger and fixed assets.

INTERNAL CONTROLS

Continue to invest in resources that maintain effective internal controls, and follow appropriate models for internal controls, such as the Federal Managers' Financial Integrity Act of 1982 (FMFIA), and the objectives on financial reporting as established under Dodd-Frank and best practices derived from OMB Circular A-123.

We will assess our progress through the following three performance goals:

Performance goal 4.3.1: Obtain an unmodified "clean" audit opinion on the CFPB's financial statements.[36]

An unmodified opinion from GAO of the CFPB's internal operations confirms that the Bureau maintains sound financial practices and robust internal controls.

PERFORMANCE MEASURE

Unmodified "clean" audit opinion on financial statements

---

36 The American Institute of Certified Public Accountant's Auditing Standards Board updated sections of the Statements of Auditing Standards with respect to the definition of the types of audit reports issue. Based on these changes, reports on audited financial statements will use the term 'unmodified opinion' instead of 'unqualified opinion' beginning in fiscal year 2013.

Targets

Target for FY 2013: Unmodified audit opinion
Target for FY 2014: Unmodified audit opinion
Target for FY 2015: Unmodified audit opinion

Actuals

Actual result for FY 2012: Unqualified audit opinion
Actual result for FY 2013: Unmodified audit opinion

PROGRESS UPDATE AND FUTURE ACTION

The CFPB has received an unmodified opinion from the GAO on its FY 2013 financial statements. GAO also previously provided unqualified opinions on the Bureau's FY 2012 and 2011 financial statements. These opinions confirm that the CFPB has implemented effective internal control over the efficiency of operations, compliance with laws and regulation, and financial reporting. The CFPB will continue to maintain a robust internal control framework over operations and financial reporting.

Performance goal 4.3.2: Award 90% of contracts competitively.

Competing procurement actions allow for competitive market pricing, stronger proposal submissions, and a distributed vendor base in support of the Bureau. Public value is also derived as money is being spent effectively.

PERFORMANCE MEASURE

TABLE 39: Percentage of contracts competitively awarded

	FY 2012	FY 2013	FY 2014	FY 2015
Target	NA	90%	90%	90%
Actual	93%	83%	NA	NA

PROGRESS UPDATE AND FUTURE ACTION

The CFPB is currently tracking competition and reporting data measurements within the agency on a quarterly basis.

At 90% the CFPB's competition goals for FY 2013 through FY 2015 are ambitious but realistic and designed to position the Bureau as a leader-by-example in stewarding public money. The CFPB does not aim for 100% competition, as the Bureau has a range of routine exempt service and supply needs, including follow-on efforts for web programming and cloud infrastructure support, witness services, conferences, and subscriptions. In addition, the Office of Procurement partners with the OMWI to develop tools and resources for increasing opportunities to minority owned and women owned businesses.

In FY 2013, out of approximately $101 million that CFPB awarded in contracts, $84 million, or 83%, were awarded on a competitive basis. By volume of contracts, 78% were awarded competitively.

CFPB's Office of Procurement met the target of 90% competitive awards for 45% of the total procurement dollars that are managed internally. The CFPB utilizes the Bureau of the Fiscal Service (BFS) for contracting support covering the remaining 55% of the procurement spend. BFS has a higher rate of direct awards, thus driving the overall percentage of contracts competitively awarded in FY 2013 to 78%.

The CFPB will continue working strenuously inside the agency, as well as with the BFS partners, to bring percentage of competitive awards in line with our ambitious goals for FY 2014 and FY 2015.

Performance goal 4.3.3: Distribute funds collected through enforcement actions to identified victims within 24 months.

This goal tracks the disbursement of CPF payments and Bureau-administered redress funds to eligible identified victims within 24 months of identifying victims. The Dodd-Frank Act authorizes the CFPB to enforce Federal consumer financial laws. Under this authority, the CFPB litigates cases which may result in redress to harmed consumers. In some cases, the Bureau will be responsible for obtaining redress funds from the defendant and distributing those funds to the harmed consumers. In addition, the Dodd-Frank Act gives the Bureau the authority to obtain civil money penalties in enforcement actions and to deposit those penalties in the Civil Penalty Fund. It may then use amounts in the Civil Penalty Fund for payments to the victims of activities for which civil penalties have been imposed.

PERFORMANCE MEASURE

Percentage of funds collected through the enforcement of Federal consumer financial laws that is distributed within 24 months of identifying victims.

Targets

FY 2013: Baseline
FY 2014: TBD
FY 2015: TBD

Actuals

FY 2012: NA (the Bureau did not collect redress funds on behalf of victims in FY 2012)
FY 2013: Baseline under development

PROGRESS UPDATE AND FUTURE ACTION

In FY 2013, the Bureau took several key steps to build the infrastructure necessary to effectively distribute redress and Civil Penalty Fund payments to eligible victims. Efforts included the hiring of appropriate Bureau staff, the establishment of a formal Civil Penalty Fund allocation process, and the hiring of vendors to manage distributions to victims. In November 2013, the Bureau began distributing Civil Penalty Fund and redress funds to eligible consumers.

Outcome 4.4: *Increase public confidence in consumer financial markets by maintaining the CFPB's transparency, accountability, and meaningful channels for feedback.*

Outcome leader: Associate Director, External Affairs

Since transparency is at the core of how the CFPB operates, the CFPB will provide clear information both on the use of resources and on its performance. To that end, the CFPB will communicate substantively and frequently across a wide range of external stakeholders, including industry and consumer groups. The CFPB aims to actively engage all stakeholders that could potentially be affected by the Bureau, with the understanding that there is much insight to be gained from varied stakeholders representing distinct points of view.

This outcome will be accomplished through the following strategies and investments:

Strategies

- Gather input from stakeholders on the CFPB's policies and operations to ensure the Bureau is effectively communicating its activities, meeting transparency goals, and actively soliciting feedback.

- Enhance program efficiency through regular analysis of operations data.

- Maintain and enhance a highly effective and usable online presence that supports multiple digital services.

Investments

EXTERNAL STAKEHOLDER ENGAGEMENT

External Affairs' budgets for FY 2014 and FY 2015 reflect investments to increase capacity to allow the Bureau to solicit a broader range of perspectives from a wider variety of stakeholders, to further amplify the Bureau's work externally, and to coordinate, support, and inform the work of the Bureau. External Affairs plans to continue to host public events in each of fiscal years 2014 and 2015 consistent with its strategic plan, to ensure that stakeholders and the public are informed about the Bureau's work and that the Bureau hears input and feedback from a diverse range of external stakeholders.

We will assess our progress through the following performance goal:

Performance goal 4.4.1: Engage the public by hosting public field hearings, town hall meetings, Consumer Advisory Board meetings, and other events on consumer finance issues.

The CFPB aims to engage with the public on consumer finance issues (a) to ensure that consumers and interested parties have visibility into the Bureau's work and have meaningful opportunities to share input publicly and (b) to ensure that the Bureau's work is informed by regular input from varied perspectives representing distinct points of view.

PERFORMANCE MEASURE

Number of public field hearings, town hall meetings, Consumer Advisory Board meetings, and other public events hosted annually

Targets

FY 2013: 8 Events
FY 2014: 9 Events
FY 2015: 9 Events

Actual

FY 2012: 8 Events
FY 2013: 11 Events

PROGRESS UPDATE AND FUTURE ACTION

The Bureau held 11 public events in FY 2013 focused on key issues affecting consumer financial markets such as mortgages, debt collection, and student financial products. These included three meetings of its Consumer Advisory Board (CAB).

1. Seattle field hearing in October of 2012 on debt collection

2. Silicon Valley public event in November of 2012 on Project Catalyst

3. Baltimore field hearing in January of 2013 on Qualified Mortgages

4. Atlanta field hearing in January of 2013 on mortgage servicing

5. Washington DC CAB meeting in February of 2013

6. Des Moines field hearing in March of 2013 on consumer complaints

7. Los Angeles CAB meeting in May of 2013

8. Miami field hearing in May of 2013 on student lending

9. Portland, Maine field hearing in July of 2013 on debt collection

10. Itta Bena, Mississippi CAB meeting and public panel discussion in September 2013

11. Washington DC public forum in September of 2013 on college banking products

The Bureau also participated in dozens of public events hosted by others, including testifying before Congress on 16 occasions during FY 2013 to discuss policy, operations and budget matters. In FY 2014 and beyond, the Bureau will continue to host events on issues impacting financial consumers, including mortgages, student loans, and other issues. The Bureau will also continue to testify on important issues at the request of Congress.

APPENDIX A:

Program evaluations

The CFPB has an expansive, vital mission yet limited resources to achieve its goals. Our vision helps to guide us in the right direction; our values set expectations for how we get there; and our strategy helps to focus our energies on areas that offer the greatest potential impact.

It is also important for us to step back, evaluate our recent past performance, and plan for that which is to come. In order to ensure the Bureau's programs and strategies are effectively achieving its goals, the Bureau uses a variety of processes and reports to periodically evaluate its performance and course correct when necessary.

GOVERNMENT ACCOUNTABILITY OFFICE

The GAO conducts studies or investigations related to the CFPB's programs every year. In FY 2012, GAO's reports included studies on the benefits and costs associated with implementing the Dodd-Frank Act; the Dodd-Frank Act's impact on community banks and credit unions, troubled mortgages and the Troubled Asset Relief Program; and, the operations of the Financial Stability Oversight Council and the Office of Financial Research, among other areas. In addition, GAO performs an annual audit of the CFPB's financial statements and internal controls, as required by the Dodd-Frank Act.

OFFICE OF THE INSPECTOR GENERAL OF THE BOARD OF GOVERNORS OF THE FEDERAL RESERVE SYSTEM AND THE CONSUMER FINANCIAL PROTECTION BUREAU

The OIG is an independent oversight authority within the Board of Governors of the Federal Reserve System that conducts audits, inspections, evaluations, and other reviews of programs and operations of the CFPB and investigations into allegations of potential misconduct by staff or contractors. The mission of the OIG is to detect fraud, waste and abuse, and to promote integrity, economy, efficiency and effectiveness in the CFPB's programs and operations. The OIG's audit reports are available on the OIG's website.

INDEPENDENT PERFORMANCE AUDIT

In accordance with the Dodd-Frank Act, the CFPB orders an annual independent audit of the operations and budget of the Bureau. The purpose of this audit is to provide objective analyses to improve program performance and operations, reduce costs, facilitate decision-making, and contribute to public accountability. The audits for prior years are available on the Bureau's website.

On a quarterly basis, the CFPB executives, including all Goal Leaders, review progress toward achieving the Bureau's strategic goals and outcomes, in part using the performance goals and measures outlined in this plan. At these points, course corrections are made as needed.

External consultation

In accordance with statute, the Bureau sought input from Congress on its Strategic Plan several times during the drafting process. In addition, the Bureau posted the Strategic Plan on its website for 30 days in order to give the public the opportunity to provide comments.

Verification of performance data

The CFPB will strive to ensure that the information reported in performance documents and the processes used to develop that information are complete and reliable. As an example of existing validation and verification processes, the Bureau is subject to an annual independent audit of operations and budget, as required by Sec. 1573 of Public Law 112–10, which includes a review of the CFPB's performance-based budgeting processes and data validation and verification policy and procedures.

In its FY 2013–2017 Strategic Plan, the CFPB is establishing a number of new performance measures in order to assess progress. In some instances, the Bureau does not have sufficient data in order to set targets for FY 2014 and FY 2015. In these cases, the Bureau either has already established or will establish baselines by the end of FY 2014, and set targets starting in FY 2014 and 2015 as applicable.

External factors

Key external factors beyond the Bureau's control have the potential to impact the CFPB's ability to effectively achieve its strategic goals and objectives.

It is anticipated that markets in both the U.S. and foreign financial services sectors will evolve over time. These future changes must be monitored, as they will impact the work of the CFPB in protecting consumers and addressing a continually changing financial environment.

Additional external factors are discussed throughout the Strategic Plan in the context of our goals and outcomes.

Management challenges

The United States Congress, in implementing the Dodd-Frank Act, followed a long-established precedent and provided the CFPB with funding outside of the congressional appropriations process to ensure full independence as the Bureau supervises and regulates providers of consumer financial products and services and protects consumers. Congress has consistently provided for independent funding for bank supervisors to allow for long-term planning and the execution of complex initiatives and to ensure that banks are examined regularly and thoroughly for compliance with the law.

The CFPB supervises over 100 very large depository institutions, including the largest, most complex banks in the country. In addition, it has been charged by Congress with responsibility for supervising thousands of nonbank providers of consumer financial products and services. Effective supervision that assures a level playing field between bank and nonbank institutions requires dedicated and predictable resources, and independent examiners.

Although Congress provided the CFPB with a source of funding outside the appropriations process, the CFPB is nonetheless the only bank supervisor with a statutory cap on its primary source of funding. If the Director were to determine that the non-appropriated funds to which it is entitled under the Dodd-Frank Act are insufficient to carry out its responsibilities, section 1017 (e) of the Dodd-Frank Act authorizes the CFPB to also obtain appropriated funds through FY 2014, up to a capped amount and subject to apportionment. In accordance with the Dodd-Frank Act and appropriations law requirements, further action would be required on the part of the Director and Congress in order for the CFPB to obtain such appropriated funds. These additional funds would be subject to apportionment under section 1517 of Title 31, United States Code, and restrictions that generally apply to the use of appropriated funds in Title 31, United States Code, and other laws.

APPENDIX B: ORGANIZATIONAL CHART

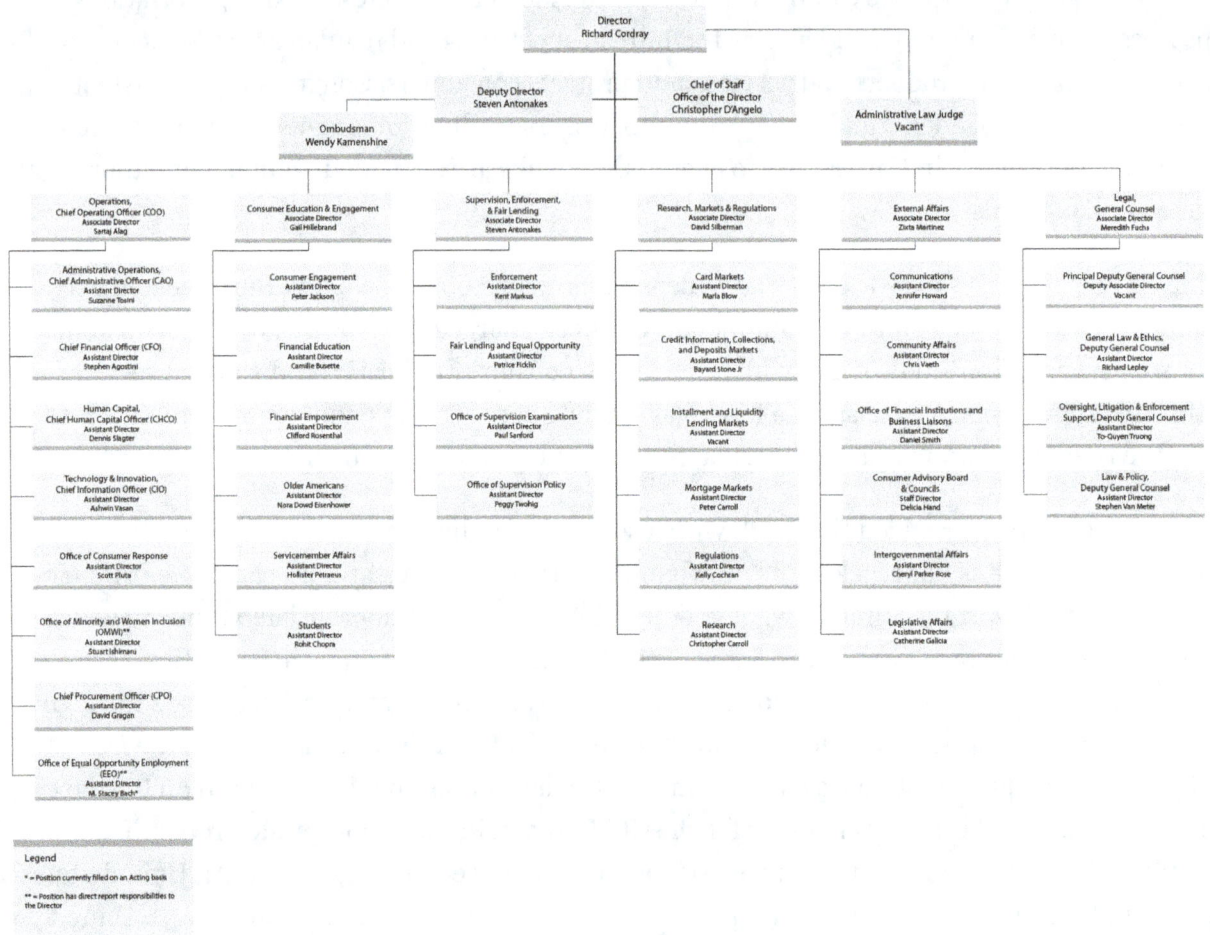

Last updated: December 10, 2013

www.ingramcontent.com/pod-product-compliance
Lightning Source LLC
Chambersburg PA
CBHW081835170526
45167CB00007B/2807